THE GREENING
OF PSYCHOANALYSIS

Croagnes, 84490 Saint-Saturnin-lès-Apt, France,
December 1997.

THE GREENING
OF PSYCHOANALYSIS

André Green's New Paradigm
in Contemporary Theory and Practice

Edited by

Rosine Jozef Perelberg & Gregorio Kohon

Foreword by
Hannah Browne & Anna Streeruwitz

KARNAC

First published in 2017 by
Karnac Books
118 Finchley Road
London NW3 5HT

British Library Cataloguing in Publication Data

A C.I.P. for this book is available from the British Library

ISBN: 978–1–78220–562–3

Edited, designed, and produced by Communication Crafts

Printed in Great Britain

www.karnacbooks.com

To the memory of

André Green

1927–2012

CONTENTS

ACKNOWLEDGEMENTS

We are grateful to the *International Journal of Psychoanalysis* for permission to reproduce, with adaptations, R. J. Perelberg, "Negative Hallucinations, Dreams and Hallucinations: The Framing Structure and Its Representation in the Analytic Setting", *IJP*, vol. 97 (No. 6): 1575–1590; to the *British Journal of Psychotherapy*, for permission to quote extensively from R. J. Perelberg, "Feelings and Their Absence from the Analytic Setting", *BJP*, 12 (1995): 212–221; and to Les Editions d'Ithaque, for permission to quote from Fernando Urribarri, *Dialoguer aver André Green. La psychoanalyse contemporaine chemin faisant* (Ithaque, 2013). We would also like to thank DACS for their kind permission to reproduce the artwork of Eduardo Chillida included in this volume.

We are both very grateful to Klara and Eric King for their help in editing the book.

ABOUT THE EDITORS AND CONTRIBUTORS

Hannah Browne did her medical training at the University of Cape Town before moving to London where she trained as a Child and Adolescent Psychiatrist at the Tavistock Clinic. A Member of the British Psychoanalytical Society, she now lives in Belfast where she combines working in the NHS with a part-time private psychoanalytic practice. She has recently completed an introductory chapter for the forthcoming edition of *British Psychoanalysis: An Independent Tradition*, edited by Gregorio Kohon.

Litza Guttieres-Green is a psychiatrist and psychoanalyst and a Training Analyst of the Paris Psychoanalytical Society. She has written on hysteria, psychic pain, and the feminine. Her papers include "Evolution of the Transference in a Case of Homosexuality Declined" (1991), in the *International Journal of Psychoanalysis*; "Le tombeau vide, douleur de l'oubli" (1991) and "Hystérie éternelle, encore et toujours" (2003), in the *Revue Française de Psychanalyse*; and "De la Douleur somatique à la douleur psychique. Discussion du cas de Marina Papageorgiou" (1999), "Maladie et masochisme. Quels rapports?" (2000), and "Hystérie et soma" (2004), in the *Revue Française de Psychosomatique*.

Gregorio Kohon is a Training Analyst of the British Psychoanalytical Society and works in London in private practice. He edited *The British School of Psychoanalysis: The Independent Tradition* (1986), and *The Dead Mother: The Work of André Green* (1999). He also published *No Lost Certainties to Be Recovered* (1999), *Love and Its Vicissitudes* (co-authored with André Green, 2005), and *Reflections on the Aesthetic Experience: Psychoanalysis and the Uncanny* (2015). His novel *Papagayo Rojo, Pata de Palo* [Red Parrot, Wooden Leg] (2007, 2008) was a finalist in the 2001 Fernando Lara Prize Planeta. He has also published, in Spanish, four books of poetry and, in 2015, a collection of short stories, *Truco Gallo* (co-authored with Mario Flecha and Viqui Rosenberg). His new book, *British Psychoanalysis: An Independent Tradition*, is to be published in the New Library of Psychoanalysis.

Michael Parsons is a Fellow and Training Analyst of the British Psychoanalytical Society and a member of the French Psychoanalytical Association. His first degree was in philosophy and classical literature & history at Oxford University. He then became a doctor and worked for some years as a hospital psychiatrist. Alongside this, he trained as an analyst at the Institute of Psychoanalysis in London and went on to spend thirty years in full-time psychoanalytic practice. He is well known internationally as a teacher and lecturer and has a particular interest in the relation between psychoanalysis and other cultural areas, such as literature, art, philosophy, and religion. He is co-editor of *Before I Was I: Psychoanalysis and the Imagination. Collected Papers of Enid Balint* (1993) and the author of two books: *The Dove that Returns, The Dove that Vanishes: Paradox and Creativity in Psychoanalysis* (2000) and *Living Psychoanalysis: From Theory to Experience* (2014).

Rosine Jozef Perelberg is a Fellow of the British Psychoanalytical Society, Visiting Fellow in the Psychoanalysis Unit at University College London, and Corresponding Member of the Paris Psychoanalytical Society. Previously she undertook a PhD in Social Anthropology at the London School of Economics. In 2011–12 she was Visiting Professor at the San Francisco Center for Psychoanalysis and in the following year Visiting Professorial Fellow at

Birkbeck, University of London. Her publications include *Psychoanalytic Understanding of Violence and Suicide* (1997), *Female Experience: Four Generations of British Women Psychoanalysts on Work with Women* (with Joan Raphael-Leff) (1998, 2008), *Freud: A Modern Reader* (2006), *Time and Memory* (2007), *Dreaming and Thinking* (2000), *Time, Space and Phantasy* (2008), and *Murdered Father, Dead Father: Revisiting the Oedipus Complex* (2015). She is currently editing a book with papers by French and British psychoanalysts, entitled *Psychic Bisexuality: A British–French Dialogue*, which will be published in the New Library of Psychoanalysis. In 2007 she was named one of the ten women of the year by the Brazilian National Council of Women. She works in private practice in London.

Jed Sekoff is on the faculties of the San Francisco Center for Psychoanalysis, the Psychoanalytic Institute of Northern California, where he is a supervising and training analyst, and the Wright Institute, Berkeley, California. For a decade he served as the Director of Psychological Medicine at the Department of Family and Community Medicine, University of Miami. He was a board member, as well as a supervising clinician, at Survivors International, a San Francisco-based agency dedicated to the treatment of torture survivors. His writings and presentations have touched on the intersection of psychoanalysis with cinema, theatre, art, and social theory, along with a clinical focus on primitive mental states, the body, and modes of therapeutic action. His publications include chapters in Gregorio Kohon, *The Dead Mother* (1999), Barry Richards, *The Crisis of the Self* (1989), and Andrea Sabbadini, *The Couch and the Silver Screen* (2003). He has served as resident commentator at two San Francisco theatre companies.

Anna Streeruwitz is a psychoanalyst of the British Psychoanalytical Society. She trained as a medical doctor at the University of Vienna, Austria. She then trained and worked as a psychiatrist at the Maudsley Hospital and at the Anna Freud Centre, London. She holds an MSc in Theoretical Psychoanalytic Studies from University College London. She works in London, in private practice.

Fernando Urribarri is an Associate Member of the Argentinian Psychoanalytic Association, where he has coordinated the André Green seminar since 2001. He is Lecturer at Buenos Aires University and Visiting Professor at Paris VII and Paris X universities and at Columbia University in New York. As a friend and student of André Green, he collaborated with Green in the preparation of several of his books, from *Key Ideas in Contemporary Psychoanalysis* (2001) to his final (posthumous) volume, *La Clinique psychanalytique contemporaine* (2012). These many years of collaboration are reflected in the book, *Dialoguer avec André Green* (2013), in which six interviews that took place between 1991 and 2011 are published.

PREFACE

In December 2014, the Scientific Committee of the British Psychoanalytical Society invited the two of us to devise an event
in honour of André Green. We proposed a whole day of papers
presented by contemporary psychoanalysts who had been inspired
by his works, which was announced as The Greening of Psychoanalysis.[1] It took place on 18 September 2015, at the British
Psychoanalytical Society. We were honoured to have the following
speakers: Litza Guttieres-Green, from France; Jed Sekoff, from the
United States; Fernando Urribarri, from Argentina, and Michael
Parsons, from the United Kingdom. We both also presented papers.
Jan Abram, the Chair of the Scientific Committee, opened the event.
It was a memorable homage to a memorable psychoanalytic giant.
We are very pleased to be able to publish the various texts in the
present volume. Our thanks to the Scientific Committee, and to
Rachel Chaplin, who helped us to organise this event.

Rosine Jozef Perelberg writes:

Although familiar with his work, I only met André Green personally in 1995, when I was invited to discuss his work on affect

xv

(*Le Discours vivant*; Green, 1973) at a conference organised by the Freud Museum at the French Institute; the proceedings were published in the *British Journal of Psychotherapy* (Perelberg, 1995). This book was untranslated at the time and was, therefore, not accessible to most of the British audience. This event marked the beginning of a friendship that lasted until the end of Green's life. His flat at Avenue de l'Observatoire became a meeting point for clinical and theoretical discussions. In 1997, the year I was appointed a Training Analyst of the British Psychoanalytical Society, André first invited me to present a paper at a scientific meeting of the Société Psychanalytique de Paris (SPP—the Paris Psychoanalytical Society). This was followed by further invitations to present my work at a number of internal and external conferences organised by the Paris Psychoanalytical Society. Some other memorable moments include the dialogue with Daniel Stern organised by Joseph Sandler at University College London (Sandler, Sandler, & Davies, 2000); the 2004 Colloquium in Cerisy-la-Salle Castle (Perelberg, 2005; Richard & Urribarri, 2005), the only time when the famous castle offered a conference on a living psychoanalyst; the closing dialogue at the 2005 European Psychoanalytical Federation Congress in Vilamoura on Interpretation and Constructions in Psychoanalysis; and the 2006 Conference on the Dead Father, at Columbia University in New York (Kalinich & Taylor, 2009; Perelberg, 2009a, 2009b). The dialogue on the Unity and Diversity of Contemporary Psychoanalysis, an open day organised by the Paris Psychoanalytical Society in January 2006 and published later as a book (Green, 2006; see also Perelberg, 2006), attracted 900 participants in Maison de la Chimie in Paris. In the summer of 2007, André Green offered a seminar in Paris on the concept of the death instinct, and he spoke for some nine hours over one weekend to an international audience of invited psychoanalysts (Green, 2007a).

I have so many memories of André, in all these different locations and countries. I particularly loved the days in Cerisy-la-Salle Castle. Over the period of four days he had a one-hour dialogue with each of the invited participants. On the final morning, the sun broke through the clouds after four days of relentless rain. We had all met in the main hall to listen to him—he was supposed to speak about his thoughts on the numerous presentations over the long weekend. He said that he felt moved and fulfilled, that his work had found resonance in our own work. We should now enjoy the sun and go into the garden. . . . I don't think there was a dry pair of eyes at that moment in the audience.

This is just one illustration of the light and the warmth André Green also gave to us.

Gregorio Kohon writes:

Although I had started reading André Green's work from the late 1960s, in Spanish translations published in Argentina, I only met him for the first time in 1993, in Brisbane, Australia. Valli, my wife, and I had invited him to participate in the Third International Conference organised by the Brisbane Centre for Psychoanalytic Studies, which we founded and directed. This time the theme was Psychoanalysis, Madness and the Theatre. André presented a paper on "Scenes of Tragic Madness in Ancient Greece", yet another example of his intellectual talent and range. We developed a strong friendship, and he remained a loyal friend and a generous colleague to the end of his life. André Green had many good friends internationally and in the British Psychoanalytical Society, across different generations. He was always willing to enter into a dialogue—not always cordial, at all times passionate—with everybody. After we returned to live in London in 1995, we had the opportunity of visiting him many times in Paris. I will never forget the special time spent at Green's house in the Luberon in December 1997, when I interviewed him over several evenings. I also had the privilege of being invited later to present clinical material in his seminar in Paris. In 2000, he asked me to become part of an international group, sponsored by the International Psychoanalytical Association, doing clinical research on borderline phenomena. The participants were Otto F. Kernberg and William I. Grossman (United States); Jaime M. Lutenberg and Fernando Urribarri (Argentina); André Green and Jean-Claude Rolland (France), and Elizabeth Bott Spillius and myself (United Kingdom). Between January 2000 and September 2003, in long, intense end-of-week clinical meetings, in an atmosphere of friendly collaboration, all of us had the opportunity of witnessing André's extraordinary clinical acumen, his psychoanalytic sensitivity, his generous and exceptional knowledge, and his helpful theoretical clarity (see Green, 2007b).

Green considered Lacan, Bion, and Winnicott his most inspiring teachers. In recognition of the very special relationship that he had with the British Psychoanalytical Society, he was invited by the late Joseph Sandler to be the Freud Memorial Professor at University College London (1979–1980); a few years later, he was made an Honorary Member of the British Psychoanalytical Society.

A particular memory stayed with me. After the 1993 conference in Brisbane, we had the opportunity to spend four days by the sea. The main beach in Noosa Heads, on the Sunshine coast, is safe, and we all had a good time swimming. On the second day, we hired a boat and crossed the river, landing on the North Shore; there, the surf is dangerous, with rough currents that can be difficult to negotiate; the presence of sharks and even poisonous sea-snakes does not make it any easier. Following the example of the locals, we had never dared to swim in that sea. Contemplating the waves, André said: "This is more like it!" He was 64 years old. Although we warned him of the dangers, he insisted that he wanted to swim. André waded cautiously into the water, trying not to lose his balance. Feeling rather responsible for his safety, I followed him. Clearly, swimming was out of the question. André, humbled, squatted down and gave himself a splash. Back on the boat, he joked: "Well, another sea conquered!"

Note

1. This title was inspired by "The Greening of Psychoanalysis: André Green in Dialogues with Gregorio Kohon" (Kohon, 1999).

References

Green, A. (1973). *Le Discours vivant. La conception psychanalytique de l'affect*. Paris: Presses Universitaires de France. [*The Fabric of Affect and Psychoanalytic Discourse*. London: Routledge, 1999.]

Green, A. (2006). *Unité et diversité des pratiques du psychanalyste*. Paris: Presses Universitaires de France.

Green, A. (2007a). *Pourquoi les pulsions de destruction ou de mort?* Paris: Editions du Panama.

Green, A. (Ed.) (2007b). *Resonance of Suffering: Countertransference in Non-Neurotic Structures*. London: Karnac.

Kalinich, L. J., & Taylor, S. W. (Eds.) (2009). *The Dead Father: A Psychoanalytic Inquiry*. London: Routledge.

Kohon, G. (1999). The Greening of psychoanalysis: André Green in dialogues with Gregorio Kohon. In: G. Kohon (Ed.), *The Dead Mother: The Work of André Green* (pp. 10–58). London: Routledge.

Perelberg, R. J. (1995). Feelings and their absence from the analytic setting. *British Journal of Psychotherapy, 12*: 212–221.

Perelberg, R. J. (2005). Jeux d'identification dans la violence. In: F. Richard & F. Urribarri (Eds.), *Autour de l'œuvre d'André Green* (pp. 95–108). Paris: Presses Universitaires de France.

Perelberg, R. J. (2006). Psychanalyse en Grande-Bretagne. In: *Unité et diversité des pratiques du psychanalyste* (pp. 41–54). Paris: Presses Universitaires de France.

Perelberg, R. J. (2009a). The dead father and the sacrifice of sexuality. In L. J. Kalinich & S. W. Taylor (Eds.), *The Dead Father: A Psychoanalytic Inquiry* (pp. 121–132). London: Routledge.

Perelberg, R. J. (2009b). Murdered father, dead father: Revisiting the Oedipus complex. *International Journal of Psychoanalysis, 90*: 713–732.

Richard, F., & Urribarri, F. (Eds.) (2005). *Autour de l'oeuvre d'André Green*. Paris: Presses Universitaires de France.

Sandler, J., Sandler, A.-M., & Davies, R. (Eds.) (2000). *Clinical and Observational Psychoanalytic Research: Roots of a Controversy*. London: Karnac.

Reflections on
The Greening of Psychoanalysis Conference

Hannah Browne & Anna Streeruwitz

O n 18 and 19 September 2015, we attended The Greening of Psychoanalysis Conference at Byron House in London. This highly successful conference was organised by the Scientific Committee of the Institute of Psychoanalysis as an international homage to André Green, who had died in 2012, aged 84. In writing our reflections on this conference for the *Bulletin of the British Psychoanalytical Society,* we expressed the hope that a book might follow. This would encourage a wider audience to engage with Green's ideas as well as with those of the speakers. Green's ideas are complex and, as with Freud, need to be returned to again and again. It is striking that, although André Green is one of the most influential analytic thinkers of the last half-century, who cites Winnicott and Bion as his most major influences after Freud, he is only touched on fleetingly, if at all, during our psychoanalytic training.[1]

We are delighted that the papers from this conference are now being published, not least because it gives us an opportunity to revisit the ideas from the conference and to engage with them further. We are greatly helped in this by the addition of Rosine Perelberg's Introduction, "André Green: The Arborescence of a Conceptual Paradigm", in which she outlines the key concepts developed by Green, emphasising the centrality of his work with borderline patients in the evolution of his ideas. This work led him to focus his thinking on the importance of affect and its relationship with representation. Perelberg traces the roots of Green's key concepts in Freud and shows how his formulations integrate ideas from diverse thinkers in the French and British psychoanalytic traditions. This "process of arborescence, with the concepts undergoing organic growth and forming an ever-expanding whole" is the essence of the Greening of psychoanalysis. This comprehensive, scholarly introduction provides an invaluable framework with which to understand Green's unique contributions, which are expanded in the subsequent papers.

Litza Guttieres-Green, André Green's widow, outlines in chapter 1, "On the Death and Destructive Drives", her thinking about ever-recurring human destructiveness and the death drive, which are key themes from Green's final book, *Illusions and Disillusions of Psychoanalytic Work* (2011).

In chapter 2, "Negative Hallucinations, Dreams and Hallucinations: The Framing Structure and Its Representation in the Analytic Setting", Rosine Perelberg uses vivid clinical material to elucidate the importance of this concept for our clinical work. The framing structure refers to the baby's introjected experience of being held by the mother: the psychic imprint of her arms (a negative hallucination) provides the framing structure that, when the mother is absent, allows an intermediate position between presence and loss to be held, which is where representation can take place. In Perelberg's detailed, terrifying, and ultimately moving account, we come to an understanding of what happens when this framing structure does not hold, due to the traumatic intrusion of a terrifying mother: the psychic disintegration that follows cannot be represented. The work of the analysis is to help the patient "to turn hallucinations into words . . . and death into absence" and, in the *après-coup* of the analysis, to allow representation of the trauma for the first time.

Jed Sekoff's chapter "Troubled Bodies: Hypochondria, Transformation and the Work of the Negative", effortlessly interweaves Green's theoretical concepts with personal anecdotes, art, and material from a single session to give a richly textured picture of hypochondria. He reminds us of our troubled relationship with our bodies, a source of anxiety and terror, hypochondriacal concerns being part of the human condition. In the hypochondriac, this becomes a static state as they refuse representation, denying a bridge between body and mind in an unconscious attempt at containment, a way of trying to guarantee continuity. It is only when we can accept change, uncertainty, and loss through the work of the negative that we are able to transform and be more fully alive.

Gregorio Kohon's chapter, "The Negative in the Work of Eduardo Chillida", draws our attention to the commonality of experience between psychoanalysis and aesthetics through an evocative exploration of the work of Edward Chillida and Richard Serra, among others. Their sculptures challenge the viewer to actively engage with time and space, form and void, internal and external, and with how to represent what cannot be represented—themes that have prominence in the work of André Green. To do so, viewers have to allow their own inner selves to become the object of exploration, and it is this that ultimately gives the work its meaning. This resonates with the uncanny and dislocating experiences of analyst and patient as they struggle to form meaning, to allow absence and presence, and to find a sense of self when the self is always other.

In chapter 5, "Intellectual Generosity: The Greekness of Green", Michael Parsons explores Green's reading of three different versions of the *Oresteia* and how this developed his thinking about the Oedipus complex and helped him to elaborate other aspects of the tragic structure at the centre of psychic life. Parsons, whose first degree was in the classics, makes a strong argument for psychoanalysts to read classic tragedies and to remain involved in conversations about myth, as these can enrich our understanding of what we encounter on the analytic stage.

Chapter 6 is a transcript of Fernando Urribarri's interview with Green in 2011, filmed using an iPhone. Initially, André Green describes his participation in the Paris Psychoanalytical Society and his relationship with Jacques Lacan. As he began to diverge from Lacan, Green found new material for thought in the British tradition of psychoanalysis, which offered a more clinical approach. Green explains how he felt that the absence of a drive model in Lacanian thinking was problematic, both in reflecting Freud's work and for clinical practice. He then outlines his own theoretical thinking on his clinical work with non-psychotic patients. Readers are deprived of the immediacy of seeing and hearing André Green speak about his ideas but will still gain an insight into his intellectual depth and breadth.

Chapter 7, "The Extension of the Psychoanalytic Field: Towards a New Contemporary Paradigm", is Fernando Urribarri's overview of the development of Green's analytic thinking and the implications for contemporary psychoanalysis and future developments. Urribarri is an Argentinian psychoanalyst and a disciple of Green. He understands the frame to be both technical and metapsychological. The analytic setting allows a tertiary process to take place, which is a rebinding between primary and secondary processes through the frame, dreams, and interpretations.

What this book cannot capture is the invigorating experience of being at the conference and hearing these prominent analysts speak. Litza Guttieres-Green set the tone with her passionate account of her husband's death. All the speakers had known André Green personally, had been influenced by his ideas, and had been helped by him to develop their own psychoanalytic thinking. There was a feeling of immense loss alongside a sense of his work continuing to evolve in many different countries.

Common to all the speakers was a sense of continuing a conversation with André Green and inviting others to join in. The liveliness of the discussion and spontaneous anecdotes about children and grandchildren seemed to represent the generativity of Green's ideas and the hope that they will continue to echo and develop, branching down the generations—a true arborescence. However, this is not to ignore the presence of death and loss and destruction, which was there at the opening of the conference and in the closing discussion. This was a struggle André Green touched on in his many writings: to be able to continue to think and love and work, with death and the void always alongside.

André Green once said in an interview that the mark of a good interpretation is when the patient responds, "That makes me think of . . .", because then you know the process continues (Caldwell, 1995). This book is a testament to that.

Note

1. At the opening of the conference, Jan Abram, chair of the Scientific Committee, reminded the attendees that André Green had been a regular visiting speaker at psychoanalytic events in London since the 1980s and had been invited in 2000 to become an Honorary Member of the British Psychoanalytical Society.

References

Caldwell, L. (1995). An interview with André Green. *New Formations,* 26: 15–35.

Green, A. (2011). *Illusions and Disillusions of Psychoanalytic Work.* London: Karnac.

Introduction

André Green: the arborescence of a conceptual paradigm

Rosine Jozef Perelberg

In a paper written in 2011 for the *Revue Française de Psychanalyse*, André Green (2011b) traces the trajectory of his own work in his quest to understand the borderline patient—from the book *On Private Madness* (1986f, which in the French edition was subtitled: "Psychoanalysis of Borderline States") to his last book, *Illusions and Disillusions of Psychoanalytic Work* (2011a). In the first, the concept of the death instinct had not been mentioned. In-between the two books lies the nine-hour weekend seminar given by Green in 2007 in Paris on the death instinct, published under the title: *Pourquoi les pulsions de destruction ou de mort?* (2007b).[1]

Green regards these three texts as constituting his introduction to the general problems encountered in the treatment of borderline patients. Such patients have led to a shift in psychoanalytic formulations, to include the centrality of the absence of the object and its repercussions on the function of representation and symbolisation. One is attempting to map and understand a population of patients that cannot be understood in terms of a psychic apparatus that is full of representations in the model of the first neurotics treated by Freud in the first two phases of his work. The shift is from an *emphasis on dreams* to an *emphasis on the act*—as opposed to specific action (Green, 1986b, p. 82)—that has the function of discharge bypassing psychic reality.

The background to these formulations is to be found in Freud's work. In 1920, Freud discovered a drive that does not correspond to any representation but expresses itself in the repetition compulsion (1920g). This formulation is at the base of Green's formulations on the negative, of blank spaces without representation, of mental structures where representations have disappeared from theoretical descriptions. When dealing with borderline patients, one thinks about the compulsion to repeat—a clinical manifestation of the death drive.

Such individuals struggle with the overwhelming experience of no meaning. The major contraposition in Green's psychoanalytic formulations, which led to a paradigm shift in contemporary psychoanalysis, is no longer that between manifest and latent content, but that between meaning and no meaning (Reed, 2002, p. 344). Instead of an object representation, there is a hole in the psyche—a *nothing*, rather than a no-*thing* (a distinction that Green takes from Bion). This is the province not of symbolisation, but of absence, the realm of the "Dead Mother", to use the title of Green's seminal paper (1986c). The somatic representative of the drive is now severed from the object representation.

The study of the borderline structures brought to the fore, Green suggests, two types of anxiety: separation anxiety and intrusion anxiety, both as expressions of difficulties in the boundaries of the relationship between ego and object.

Green identifies some characteristics of the structure of such patients: retreat into the somatic; expulsions via actions; splitting rather than repression; disinvestment; and the expression of a primary depression. "Futility, lack of awareness of presence, limited contact are all expressions of the same basic emptiness that characterises the experience of the borderline person" (1986b, p. 79). The various stages in the analyses of the "Wolf Man" (Freud, 1918b [1914]) are the point of departure in Green's profound reflection about the clinical practice of psychoanalysis. Nowadays most psychoanalysts would consider this case as borderline.

Green's formulations include Freudian metapsychology, but they push psychoanalytic thinking further towards a theory of psychotic configurations and a theory of that which has not reached representation, or is of the order of the unrepresentable. It includes a theory of affect, of the drives and objects, of the disjunction between conscious and unconsciousness, of the subject and of the object, of the intrapsychic and the intersubjective, and a theory of the origins of thought itself. Thinking is related to absence, and also to sexuality. The Greenian psychoanalytic framework may be viewed as a theory of gradients, with the total theory being more important than any one of its parts (Perelberg, 2005), or as a process of arborescence, with the concepts undergoing organic growth and forming an ever-expanding whole that can be subsumed in what Green called *la pensée clinique*—clinical thinking (Green, 2002b, 2002c, 2005c). It may be that any of the terms may represent the whole, but it is the whole that needs to be looked at.

I shall retrace some of the main steps in Green's thinking, exploring some of his key contributions to the understanding of the borderline patient: affects, metapsychology, narcissism, the dead mother, the work of the negative, and the death instinct.

The borderline patient

Green's paper, "The Analyst, Symbolization and Absence in the Analytic Setting" (1975, 1986a), published as the second chapter in *On Private Madness*, is a marker in Green's formulations. It was presented in English to the 1975 IPA Congress in London and anticipates many of Green's themes that were to be developed more fully in the decades that followed: on the work of the negative, on narcissism (positive and negative), and on the implications of the treatment of the borderline patient for a theory of technique.

Green portrays the population that currently comes to analysis, the designations given by the main psychoanalytic authors, and the role of the transference and of symbolisation; he also formulates some implications for a theory of technique.

The new categories of patients coming to analysis have been characterised by different authors in various ways:

... borderline states, schizoid personalities (Fairbairn, 1940), "as if" personalities (Deutsch, 1942), disorders of identity (Erikson, 1959), ego-specific defects (Gitelson, 1958), false personality (Winnicott, 1956), and basic fault (Balint, 1968). The list grows if we also include some French contributions: pregenital structures (Bouvet, 1956), the operative thought of psychosomatic patients (Marty, de M'Uzan, & David, 1963) and the anti-analysand (McDougall, 1972). Now the narcissistic personality (Kernberg, 1970, 1974; Kohut, 1971) occupies our attention. [Green, 1986a, p. 32]

When working with such patients, the analyst's experience is that of

feeling caught in the patient's network of mummified objects, paralysed in his activity and unable to stimulate any curiosity in the patient about himself. His attempts at interpretations are treated by the patient as his madness, which soon leads the analyst to decathect his patient and to a state of inertia characterized by an echo response. [p. 38]

Green suggested that these borderline states have the same relevance to modern clinical practice as did the actual neurosis in Freud's time. He thought them as "durable organisations" but, unlike in neurosis, one could observe "the absence of infantile neurosis, the polymorphous character of the so-called adult 'neurosis' in such cases and the haziness of the transference neurosis" (1986f, p. 5).

Green identifies four main mechanisms in such patients that make them unavailable to the analytic process:

1. *Somatic exclusion:* This refers to a process of regression that dissociates the conflict from the psychic sphere by restricting it to the soma (and not to the libidinal body) through a process of separation between the psyche and the soma. Green refers here to the work of Marty, de M'Uzan and David (1963) and that of Fain (1966).

2. *Expulsion via action.* Acting out is a process, as is expelling psychic reality. These two mechanisms, according to Green, create psychic blindness. The patient blinds himself to his psychic reality—either to the somatic sources of his drive or to its point of entry into external reality, avoiding the intermediate

processes of elaboration. In both these cases, the analyst feels out of touch with his patient's psychic reality.

3. *Splitting.* The mechanism of (so-called) splitting remains in the psychic sphere. All the other defences are secondary to it.

> The effects of splitting go from a protection of a secret zone of non-contact where the patient is completely alone (Fairbairn, 1940; Balint, 1968) and where his real self is protected (Winnicott, 1960, 1963) or again which hides part of his bisexuality (Winnicott, 1971a), to attacks on linking in his thought processes (Bion, 1957, 1959, 1970; Donnet & Green, 1973) and the projection of the bad part of the self and of the object (M. Klein, 1946) with a marked denial of reality. When these mechanisms are used the analyst is in touch with psychic reality, but either he feels cut off from an inaccessible part of it or he sees his interventions crumble, being perceived as a persecutor and intruder. [Green, 1986a, p. 39]

4. *Decathexis.* Green is referring here to a radical decathexis on the part of the patient who seeks to attain a state of emptiness and aspires to non-being and nothingness. In the countertransference analysts feel themselves identified with a space devoid of objects, or find themselves outside it (1986a, p. 39). This radical decathexis engenders blank states of mind, without affective components, pain, or suffering. There is an inability to mourn or to tolerate guilt feelings.

The fundamental contradiction one identifies in such patients, Green suggests, is a duality of separation anxiety and intrusion anxiety—hence the centrality of the notions of closeness and distance (Bouvet, 1956, 1958).[2] Such patients refer the analyst to the very process of formation of thoughts and symbols, an area to which Bion's contributions are central (1957).

Donnet and Green (1973) suggest the notion of *blank psychosis*, at the core of psychotic phenomena, "characterised by blocking of thought processes, the inhibition of the functions of representations and by 'bi-triangulation' where the difference of the sexes which separates two objects disguises the splitting of a single object" (Green, 1986a, p. 40). In the oedipal structure the differentiation between mother and father is not that between the sexes, but between the good and the bad on the one hand, and nothingness on the other. The good is inaccessible, and the bad is always intrusive. "Thus we are dealing with a triangle based on the relationship between the patient and two symmetrically opposed objects which are in fact one entity. Hence the term 'bi-triangulation'" (1986a, p. 41) or tri-dyadic relationships (1986b, p. 80). The outcome of this is "paralysis of thought", expressed in negative hypochondriasis.

Green emphasises that the role of the analyst is no longer that of unveiling a hidden meaning, but one of construction of a meaning that had not been created before the analytic relationship began. In this view, he follows the French psychoanalyst, Serge Viderman (1970).

Inspired by Lacan, this leads Green to the formulation that absence "has an intermediate status, being between presence intrusion and loss. Excess of presence is intrusion; excess of absence is loss" (1986b, p. 82).

The borderline patient is unable to establish the primary difference (between inside and outside, subject and object, representation and perception). The aspect of splitting is crucial in such patients in that Yes and No coexist with "Neither-Yes-nor-No", which expresses the experience that the object is and is not real, or that "the object is neither real nor unreal (fantasied)" (1986b, p. 65; see also Kohon, 2007). It represents a "negative refusal of choice" (Green, 1986b, p. 82). The text on the Wolf Man (Freud, 1918b [1914]) becomes paradigmatic of "the wish to know nothing" (foreclosure, in Lacan's term), expressing the impossibility of deciding between the wish to experience and orgasm like the mother or like the father (Green, 1986d, p. 230). The Wolf Man is described as having a tortuous thought process, with at least two opinions at the same time; he was incapable of deciding whether something was good or bad, or whether he was a man or a woman (Green, 1999a, p. 274). Such refusal to choose, Green suggests, is ultimately a refusal to live.

Green believes that Winnicott has made the most important contribution with his concepts of "non-communication", "void", and "emptiness": such patients, for whom "the negative side of relationships predominates", are unable to create potential space.

How to account for this clinical picture? Green develops the idea of a *primitive madness* in the mother's relationship to the child that refers to the "conjunction between sexuality and love" (1986d,

p. 245). If, on the one hand, the mother needs to foster the birth of her infant's instinctual life, she needs, on the other, to help her child to process it, so that it is not overwhelmed by excitations. However, by definition, the mother oscillates between excess of gratification and excess of frustration. In this process the challenge is for the mother to modulate her own instinctual and phantasy life. If the mother is absent for too long, the child will cathect a dead object. Too much waiting leads to hopelessness and despair.

In his account on the treatment of a schizophrenic patient Kohon describes how "the fixation on this relationship with a primary object, in the initial phase of an exclusive as well as intense lasting attachment, will be the source of psychotic states and the perversions. And at the origin of all forms of love" (2005, p. 63).

The notion of the censorship of the mother as lover, introduced by Braunschweig and Fain (1975), became central to Green's formulations. The infant's identification with the mother and her desire, at the source of the beginnings of phantasy life, requires the mother, in her maternal role, to repress her identification as a lover to the father. Hélène Parat (2011) underlines the other side of this experience: that of the mother. For her, her baby is a sexual "bomb", an incessant provocateur who raises the tension of the partial drives of the woman who has become a mother. The mother awakens the infant's sexuality, but there is a dimension that comes from the mother as well. The censure of the mother-as-lover creates a prohibition for the mother herself. Parat suggests that the notion of a "well-tempered maternal erotic" under a protective superego is representative of the paternal prohibition in the symbolic order.

Green emphasises the notion of "passivation": a capacity to entrust oneself to maternal care. He suggests that the psychoanalytic process is not possible without this passivation, whereby the patient entrusts himself to the analytic care (1986d, p. 248)—something that is a challenge in the analyses of such patients.

Affect[3]

Green's conceptualisation of affect in psychoanalytic metapsychology and in clinical practice arose from his criticism of Lacan, who had taken spoken and written language as a paradigm for understanding the language of the unconscious (Green, 1977, 1986g).

Green undertook a detailed review of the way in which throughout his work Freud continuously discussed the relationship between affect and ideas as components of human experience [Perelberg, 1995, pp. 212–214]. He selected four "moments" in time from Freud's work: *The Interpretation of Dreams* (Freud, 1900a), *Papers on Metapsychology* (Freud, 1915c, 1915d, 1917d [1915], 1917e [1915], all written in 1915), *The Ego and the Id* (Freud, 1923b), and, finally, *Inhibitions, Symptoms and Anxiety* (Freud, 1926d [1925]). On these four occasions Freud fashions or refashions a global formulation of his overall conception of psychic activity.

In the first phase of his work, Freud equated affect with energy; symptoms represented the need for the mind to rid itself of large quantities of such affective energy in order to restore its equilibrium. Affect was linked to discharge, and thus the connection between affective experience and the body was stressed. Freud did not distinguish between the psychic and the somatic and discussed mainly the negative affects, such as those that denote suffering, distress, or anxiety (Stein, 1991, p. 5).

In the second period of his work, throughout the elaboration of the topographical model, three themes permeated Freud's writings: the issue of quality, the problem of the transformation of affect, and the question of unconscious affect. During this phase of his work Freud's main interest was dream symbolism and the elaboration of the mental apparatus. Thus the role of affects was secondary to that of representations, and Freud's emphasis is on the analysis of the dream contents (Green, 1973). Freud was also interested in the fluidity of affects in connection with ideas so that affects can be allowed expression, be suppressed, or be turned into their opposite. Affects become the pointers to missing thoughts: the ideational material has undergone displacements and substitutions, whereas the affects have remained unaltered. It was only in 1926 that anxiety was perceived as an affective signal, a response of the ego indicating the likely occurrence of a situation of danger (1926d [1925]). The new theory of anxiety also introduced the object into the conceptualisation of anxiety.

The energy concept, nevertheless, still remained an essential part of psychoanalytic theory in the third phase. However, by pointing out in 1926 that anxiety or fear could also arise as a consequence of the perception of danger in the real world, Freud linked affects to subjective experience, phantasy, and objects. In the same paper, Freud went further to suggest that the affects of patients in analysis were reproductions of earlier affective experiences, thus linking affect and memory.

Already in 1896 in a letter to Fliess, Freud had stated that "consciousness and memory are mutually exclusive" (Freud, 1950 [1892–1899, p. 234). Memory thus belongs to the unconscious. The task of the analyst "is to make out what has been forgotten from the traces which it [repression] has left behind or, more correctly, to construct it", as Freud suggested in his work on constructions in analysis (Freud, 1937d, p. 259). This position opened the way for the modern view that affective states that have never been put into words can be repeated and understood in the analytic experience. The notion of affect had increased in importance in Freud's work. In the structural model of the mind, with the shift from the unconscious to the id, there was a return to the importance of the drive impulses that become more independent from the ideational content.

Green distinguished between two types of affect: (1) affect that is integrated into a chain of signifiers, and (2) affect that overflows from the unconscious chain "like a river which leaves its bed and disorganizes communications, destroying sense-making structures" (1986f, p. 206). The excess of unmetabolised affect can give rise to different clinical manifestations, such as somatisation, perverse excitement, or an "over cathexis of external perception which monopolizes all psychic attention" (p. 209). Processes of dissociation and splitting may lead to the installation of a "dead space in the heart of the subject" (p. 209).

Green argues that restricting the understanding of these affective representations to unconscious phantasies is a mistake, as one should differentiate between *"chaos"* and *"nothingness"* (p. 211; italics in the original). Representation, which is the aim of a psychoanalytic process, is to be reached through a process of psychic work, where the patient is helped to establish live intrapsychic communication, and not through a process whereby the analyst communicates to the patient his unconscious phantasies.

Green introduces the notion of a *primary symbolisation*:

> Where the matrices of experience, unaware of the distinction between affect and representation, are formed on the basis of a primary logic, the expression of a minimal unconscious semantic, where we would find the figures of psychoanalytic rhetoric: repetition-compulsion, reversal (turning into the opposite and turning against the self), anticipation, mirroring, inclusion, exclusion, formation of the complement, mediation between inside and outside, the emergence of the category of the intermediary, the situation between the same and the other, the constitution of movable limits, temporary splitting, the creation of substitutes, the setting up of screens and *finally* projective identification. . . . These are the prerequisites for connections between symbolization and absence . . . [1986f, pp. 211–212]

Affect is always a "trace", "a residue, awoken by a repetition" (p. 179). Green believed that "in psychoanalysis as it is practised today, work on the affects commands a large part of our efforts. There is no favourable outcome that does not involve an affective change" (1977, p. 129, 1986f, p. 174).

Metapsychology:
drives and representations

The primacy of psychic conflict and the relation between drives and representations are the dimensions that make up Freudian metapsychology. Conflict is a requirement of the functioning of the psychic apparatus—between the self-preservative and the libidinal drives in the topographical model of the mind, and between the life and the death drives in the structural model.

The relationship between drives and representations in their different vicissitudes is a concern that permeated Freud's writings since the "Project for a Scientific Psychology" (1950 [1895]) and increased in complexity in his metapsychological papers. It is characterised by a *disjunction* that enables Freud to provide a model for the understanding of the different psychopathologies: hysteria, obsessional neurosis, and phobias, as affect and representation follow different paths in each of them. In the first the affect is discharged while the ideational content is repressed; in obsessional neurosis the ideational content is rejected and the affect disappears via a reaction formation. In phobias the ideational content is displaced and the quantitative element is transformed into anxiety (e.g., fear of the wolf instead of love for the father).

In *Instincts and Their Vicissitudes* Freud describes the vicissitudes undergone by the drives: reversal into its opposite and turning around upon the subject's own self (Freud, 1915c, p. 126). Delourmel (2013) suggests that the conceptual model of the drive dynamism of the double reversal and the work of the negative (the negative hallucination of the global apprehension of the mother) are at the basis of André Green's theorisation of his model of primary narcissism (Green, 2001, pp. 48–49).

Green refers to an internal inhibition of aim intrinsic to the nature of the sexual drive:

> Between the undifferentiated state of ego–id and mother–infant and the emergence of repression, a mediating process occurs involving a regulation of the drives. . . . The double reversal allows us to think about this mediation structurally. . . . [It concerns] the work that prevents a drive from attaining direct satisfaction, not by means of a force that is alien to it—repression as a psychological process—but by an internal modification of its own nature. [Green, 2001, pp. 79–80]

This statement, which puts an emphasis on the modulation of the drives themselves, may sound somewhat mysterious to a British analyst. It is nevertheless one of the cornerstones of Green's clinical thinking (see also Green, 1995). The primary object becomes crucial in mitigating the excess that comes from their force. How will the analyst achieve this? By constructing an analytic space in which free association and psychoanalytic listening are possible, the analyst can help the patient to create meaning and obtain relief from previously dominant but unknown terror. A gripping example is found in Green's 2000 paper on the central phobic position (2000a, discussed below).

When dealing with borderline patients, one thinks about the repetition compulsion, a clinical manifestation of the death drives, as it is conceived in most of the French psychoanalytic literature. There is an emphasis on the quantitative factor, not reducible to the domain of phantasies.

The notions of binding and unbinding are crucial here. They refer to the process whereby affect and representation become bound to each other as one goes from the unconscious system to the preconscious–conscious. In the unconscious system, energy is unbounded and mobile, and the rules of primary process, such as displacement and condensation, dominate. The pleasure principle reigns; there is an absence of thinking and a predominance of visual and sense impressions. Words are used as objects, and there is no sense of time. In the preconscious–conscious system energy becomes bounded, leading to the creation of a temporal sequence and a delay of motor discharge through secondary-process thinking.

The structural model, Green argues, reassesses the relevance of the movement and force of the drives, as it is based on the existence of mental structures where representations have disappeared from theoretical descriptions. The discovery of the compulsion to repeat radically changed the Freudian system.

With the ordinary neurotic patient, the free associative process itself allows for a process of unbinding to take place. When considering dreams, the work of interpretation is that of re-establishing a meaning that has been distorted. There is a process of work—dream work—that has taken place in order to disguise that which will be the object of interpretation: the manifest content of the dream. The dream work has transformed latent thoughts into the manifest dream content. In his *Interpretation of Dreams* (1900a), Freud searched for a normal thought, repressed and transformed by the work of primary process (Mannoni, 1968, p. 71).

With borderline and narcissistic patients, analysts are very often offered scenes that they are "nudged" to participate in. These scenes, which may be viewed as operating under the repetition compulsion, contain a closure about them that is going to be the analytic task to "undo", or to expand. This is one of the paradoxical uses that Freud makes of the notion of binding. If, on the one hand, it implies the process of establishing links in the service of the life instinct, it may, on the other hand, imply fixations. In such cases, it is the analytic task to attempt to facilitate the freeing, or opening up, of the associative chain. The analyst's task is to be receptive to the anxieties as they may be expressed in the consulting room, contain them, and be able to transform feelings and experiences into thoughts that are more bearable, so that the patient is able to think about them.

The dead mother

Green's "The Dead Mother" (1986c), initially published in 1983, constitutes a paradigm in psychoanalysis, a revisiting and expansion of many crucial concepts in the Freudian metapsychology, such as the relationship between drives and representations, primary repression, primal phantasies, narcissism, identification, mourning, the dead father, and the Oedipus complex. The dead mother complex is a concept that has penetrated French psychoanalysis and is implicitly, if not explicitly, present in much contemporary French writing (Kohon, 1999a). I have previously suggested that the dead mother complex is a core concept to the understanding of borderline psychopathology (Perelberg, 1999).

Dedicated to Green's analyst, Catherine Parat, Green's celebrated paper deals with issues of mourning. Green is not, however, concerned with the consequences of the real death of the mother,

> but rather that of an imago which has been constituted in the child's mind, following maternal depression, brutally transforming a living object, which was a source of vitality for the child, into a distant figure, toneless, practically inanimate, deeply impregnating the cathexes of certain patients whom we have in analysis, and weighing on the destiny of their object-libidinal and narcissistic future. Thus the dead mother, contrary to what one might think, is a mother who remains alive but is, so to speak, psychically dead in the eyes of the young child in her care. [Green, 1986c, p. 142]

Two ideas are central to his conceptualisation: the notion that object loss is a "fundamental moment in the structuring of the human psyche" (1986c, p. 143); and the notion of a depressive position and its formative role in the organisation of psychic apparatus, in a way that combines both Melanie Klein's and Winnicott's contributions.

Green addresses what he designates as the category of blankness:

> The category of blankness—negative hallucination, blank psychosis, blank mourning, all connected to what one might call the problem of emptiness, or to the negative, in our clinical practice—is the result of one of the components of primary repression: massive decathexis, both radical and temporary, which leaves traces in the unconscious in the form of "psychical holes". [Green, 1986c, p. 146]

It is only in the vicissitudes of the analytic process that one can have access to the dead mother, as it is *"a revelation of the transference"* (1986c, p. 148). Progressively, a *"transference depression"* expresses itself which, according to Green, is an expression of an infantile depression (p. 149). This depression *"takes place in the presence of an object that is itself absorbed by a bereavement"* (p. 149, italics in original). Many factors may have led to this depression—perhaps the loss of a loved one, a child, a husband, or some profound disappointment that leads to a "brutal change of the maternal imago, which is truly mutative" (p. 149). A basic vitality disappears—a loss of meaning for the child (p. 150). Green suggests that the child will understand this as somehow connected with the father and may turn to the father, who will be unable to respond to the child's needs.

Green indicates that this may have, as a consequence, "the decathexis of the maternal object and the unconscious identification with the dead mother" (1986c, pp. 150–151). This constitutes a "psychical murder of the object, accomplished without hatred" (p. 151).

The loss of meaning leads to a premature development of fantasmatic and intellectual capacities of the ego, with a *compulsion to imagine* and also a *compulsion to think*, to the creation of a *patched breast* that aims to mask the hole left by the decathexis (1986c, p. 152). The ego will have a hole within it from now on. The individual loses the capacity to love and to hate.

Green's paper may be considered as founding a new paradigm in psychoanalytic theory, leading to all the subsequent works that consider unpresentable states of mind: "A feeling of captivity . . . dispossesses the ego of itself and alienates it to an unrepresentable figure" (1986c, p. 152).

The paper brings forth a crucial point of technique and the consequent pitfalls:

> Manifestations of hatred and the following process of reparation are manifestations which are secondary to this central decathexis of the maternal primary object. One can understand that this view modified even analytic technique, because to limit oneself to interpreting hatred in structures which take on depressive characteristics amounts to never approaching the primary core of this constellation. [Green, 1986c, p. 146]

Green criticises the silent analyst—a practice that seemed to prevail among French psychoanalysts at the time—as it only perpetuates the experience of black mourning for the mother. He believes that the emphasis on hatred and destructiveness emphasised by the Kleinians misses the point. Green privileges Winnicott's position in the use of an object (Winnicott, 1971c) but also believes that Winnicott underestimates the role of sexual phantasies.

The challenge for the analyst is to stay alert to the associative links that are expressed in the process and to the experiences of the patient, and establish preconscious links that support tertiary processes without giving direct interpretations of unconscious phantasies (1986c, p. 163). Green is aware of the paradox of bringing the dead mother alive. The dead mother may be lost to the individual, but she is there. If she is awakened and animated in the transference, the individual loses her. The individual is caught in the dilemma: "presence in death, or absence in life" (p. 164).

Narcissism

As early as in a paper originally written in 1975, Green reflected on the centrality of the concept of narcissism as "an original cathexis of the undifferentiated ego, with no reference to unity" (1986a, p. 53). It is a structure, not a state. An important reference to Winnicott is his formulation (1963) that the real self is silent and isolated, in a

state of permanent non-communication. This is in no way pathological, as its aim is to protect that which is most essential to the
self. Winnicott goes further in his statement that "[i]t can be said
that only out of non-existence can existence start" (Winnicott, 1974).

Positive narcissism, as an encapsulated personal space, is contrasted with the negative effect that refers to states of emptiness
and nothingness (Green, 1986a, p. 55; 2002a). This will make reference not only to space, but also to time—"dead times", where
symbolisation does not take place (Green, 1986a, p. 56).

Green has suggested that narcissism is one of the fiercest forms
of resistance to analysis:

> Is it not true that defending the One involves, ipso facto, reject-
> ing the unconscious; since the latter implies that a part of the
> psyche exists which is acting in its own interests, thwarting the
> empire of the ego? [Green, 2001, p. ix]

Green has pointed out that "before narcissism, there were the
drives of self-preservation; after, there were the death drives"
(2001, p. x). The death drive, being muted, is expressed through
the repetition compulsion. It opened the way to the understanding
of that which has not yet reached symbolisation. Green has suggested the possibility of a dual narcissism: a positive narcissism,
whose aim is to reach unity, a narcissism aiming at oneness; and a
negative narcissism, which strives towards the zero level, aiming
at nothingness and moving towards psychic death, as the psyche
yearns for its own annihilation. For Green, negative narcissism is
the form narcissism takes when combined with self-destructive
drives. This way of understanding is not limited to the patients'
manifestations of destructivity, but includes states of mind where
objects are deprived of their quality of being unique or irreplace-
able for the subject (2001; see also 2002a, p. 637).

In *positive narcissism*, other people are seen as being of low
value; in *negative narcissism*, the patient is the one who is worthy
only of universal contempt. Negative narcissism allows the interpretation of certain aspects of contemporary clinical manifestations: states of void and decathexis, feeling of futility, tendency to
no-commitment, and subjective disinvolvement. It can be identified in eating disorders, where the more one tries to fill the inner
feeling of vacuity, the more one finds oneself more empty, in some

suicidal impulses, and also in drug addictions. *Death narcissism* is a culture of void, emptiness, self-contempt, destructive withdrawal, and permanent self-depreciation with a predominant masochistic quality. Green has suggested the term *disobjectalising function*, which undoes the transformation of psychic functions into objects.

Green has suggested that, instead of a fruitless debate that involves evolutionary issues around the concept of narcissism, it is much more fruitful to determine "how the different clinical configurations are organised; to recognise the nature of their internal coherence" and to identify the narcissistic transference in different types of psychopathologies.

Subject and object

Subject and object must be inserted in the context of lineages. They are like two threads, simultaneously independent and interconnected, where structures of the object and of the subject are formed (1986c, p. 156). In making this suggestion, Green views the structuring of psychic life in terms of the two great polarities that Freud proposed. Post-Freudian psychoanalysis has largely been concerned with the object, without questioning to which object one was referring. Thus one can point to the genesis of the self: the work of Hartmann, Edith Jacobson, and, later, Klein and even Winnicott used the concept of *self* (of I). Racamier added the person (or the persona, the mask), and Lacan gave the subject a central position in the theory. Later still the subjective returns in the intersubjective theories. Green prefers the position of *subjectale* lineage, which can encompass most of the propositions that have been put forward (subject, I, self, etc.), attributing to each of these ideas their field of action (p. 157).

Depending on the issue in question, the analyst refers to different concepts, without attempting to unify them. Thus Green suggests that when dealing with borderline patients, one thinks about the concept of the ego: its limits, defences, and choices of object, and its relation with the repetition compulsion. On the other hand, when one speaks of neurosis, the reference to the subject is more pertinent.

Green also points out the impossibility of arriving at a unified view of the object, and he emphasises the multiplicity of ideas connected with the object: object of phantasy, real object, object of the id, object of the ego, and so on. In psychoanalytic practice, the object is expressed mainly as the object in the transference.

Thirdness and temporality

In "Psychoanalysis and Ordinary Modes of Thought" (1986g), Green considers the relationship between primary and secondary processes, the duality established by Freud, the basis for thinking about the psychic apparatus: "the limit of the greatest possible reduction as far as intelligibility is concerned" (p. 18). This fundamental duality is the basis for establishing a relationship and the very condition for symbolisation and the production of a third party.

In 1975, Green stated: "The analytic object is neither internal (to the analysand or analyst) nor external (to one or the other), but it is in-between them" (1986e, p. 288). In a session the analytic object is like a third object, a product of the meeting of analysand and analyst. Following Freud, however, Green thinks that there has been an emphasis on "pre-oedipal" relations. It was Lacan who brought the role of the father back into the field of discussion.

Inspired by the work of Charles Sanders Peirce, Green suggests the crucial relevance of the third in psychoanalytic theory. It is not the oedipal triangle that is evoked here, but the going beyond the *here and now* via the always implied reference to the third dimension (*ailleurs* and *autrefois*), which is always marked by absence, being the present or the past, as well as the future (2004). These ideas emphasise time as crucially creating thirdness in the psychoanalytic process (Green, 2002d, 2003; Perelberg, 2006, 2008, 2013)

Green points out that Winnicott's (1971b) notion of an "intermediate area" or "potential space" played a seminal role in transforming the "two-body psychology" that was attributed to the psychoanalytic scene of the 1950s. In effect, the notion of a third space considers other spatial possibilities that exist in relation to the dialectic between two subjectivities.

The symbol has been defined as the coming together of a divided object. Green identifies three parts: each of the divided parts, plus a third, made up of the two other parts. In the sessions, he suggests, the analytic object is like a third part, the product of the union of the two parts constituted by analyst and analysand. Green refers to the symbolic in Lacan's terminology and also to Bion's work, in the suggestion that as well as the mother and the baby, it is the mother's alpha-function that expresses this thirdness in the relationship. Thirdness is present in all aspects of any thinking about the psychoanalytic models (Green, 2004, p. 118).

The implications for psychoanalysis are immense: one cannot talk about the relationship between a subject and an object (object relationship)—instead, "the three party relationship is the matrix of the mind" (p. 132).

Green regards the Oedipus complex as a structure and suggests that the historical and structural Oedipus is a model of which we only have approximations. The full extent of the Oedipus complex, with its dimensions of incest, parricide, and the creation of incestuous children, can only ever be reached in reality in one dimension and never in all its dimensions. The triangle of this structure is an open rather than a closed triangle, with a substitutable third (Green, 1992, p. 131, 2004). This contains echoes of Lacan's shift from his formulation "*le nom du père*" to "*des noms-du-père*" (Lacan, 2005). *There are multiple third dimensions that cannot be reduced to the empirical presence of the father* (Perelberg, 2009, p. 724). The other of the object, that which is not the subject, becomes the third in the oedipal situation. It is a symbolic dimension, which corresponds to the notion of the paternal metaphor in Lacan, and which is not necessarily the real person of the father. It is ultimately related to the generalisation of thought.

The work of the negative

The notion of the negative was developed by André Green in order to account for both normal and pathological processes (1999c). The negative is the very condition for the existence of the structuring psychic apparatus. Green emphasises the work of the negative in both its structuring and its destructuring functions. The outcome is determined by the equilibrium between the life and the death drives.

Repression establishes the distinctions between the unconscious and the preconscious–conscious. The unconscious is defined as the negative of the conscious: absence of time and lack of regard for the categories of contraries and contradictions.

Many crucial concepts in psychoanalytic theory are conceived of in terms of the negative: the theory of repression illustrates the work of the negative; the id is conceived in terms of the negative of the ego (Green, 2005b); splitting and denial are primarily the denial of perceptions; foreclosure; negation; splitting; disavowal. Green points out the concept of –K developed by Bion, as well as Winnicott's identification of the "negative side of relationships" (Winnicott, 1971b, p. 21).

Freud's paper "Negation" (1925h) is considered by Green as crucial in the development of this concept. In this paper, negation is a means to take cognisance of that which is repressed. Green suggests that though the paper can stand alone, it is the most important step in an exploration of a function that started much earlier.

Some precursors of the development of this notion in Freud's work are identified, starting with *The Interpretation of Dreams* (Freud, 1900a) and including *On Dreams* (1901a) and the papers on metapsychology: "Gradually, the idea of the non-existence of the No in dreams was included in a broader conception, around 1915, defining the system unconscious" (Green, 2005b, p. 255). Furthermore, "no negation, no doubt, no degrees of certainty; all this is introduced by the work of the censorship between *Ucs.* and *Pcs.*" (Freud, 1901a, p. 661). "The absence of negation is part of a larger number of related characteristics, as we find it, altogether, with other notions: no sense of time, no sense of reality" (Freud, 1915e, p. 186).

Freud considers negation in terms of its function at the beginning of the distinction between inside and outside, as it separates between me and not me. Thus, negation lies at the origin of the activity of thinking itself, as well as the capacity to symbolise.

At the beginning, when it expels everything that is felt to be unpleasurable, the infant knows nothing of the outside that it has "created", except that he has to keep it as far as he can from his inside. This situation comes to an end with separation, which imposes the realisation of the independent existence of the object. With this step, the distinction between inside and outside is finally achieved.

> The outside, which includes now all objects, good as well as bad, because of the happening of separation, induces to find once more those objects which have already existed, but only in the form of representations previously introjected (and repressed). The first move of expulsion has led to a distinction between me and not-me. [Green, 2005b, p. 261]

Green introduces the notion of the double limit with the distinctions between inside and outside (a vertical line) and, within the inside, divided in the middle, the horizontal limit between consciousness on the upper level and the unconscious on the lower level.

Green indicates his intellectual indebtedness to both Winnicott and Bion.

In an addendum to his chapter on transitional phenomena, Winnicott describes a patient who had a previous unhappy analysis and kept lamenting about it. Her comment was as follows: "The negative of him [the previous analyst] was more real than the positive of you" (1971b, p. 23). She later exclaimed: "I suppose I want something that never goes away" (p. 23). Winnicott uses this example to introduce the idea that for certain patients who had traumatic experiences of separation, only the negative is real: the only reality is that which is not there. Winnicott concludes that when the experience of separation is prolonged beyond the tolerance of the child, a process of disinvestment takes place, and the object ends up disappearing from the psyche, giving rise to the experience of void and emptiness.

In a moving example, Winnicott comments in a footnote about his contact with a mother, ten years after he had seen her as a child. The mother commented that "she felt the most important separation to have been his loss of her when she was seriously depressed; it was not just her going away, she said, but her lack of contact with him because of her complete preoccupation with other matters" (Winnicott, 1971b, p. 17). This may be understood as a precursor to Green's notion of the dead mother.

There are other ideas on the negative in Winnicott's paper, Green argues, that do not belong to pathology. When Winnicott defines the "*not*-me possession", he is suggesting a concept of object that is distinguished from its usual definition either as a need-satisfying object, as an object of desire, or as a fantasised object. The definition emphasises the negative of me. Green believes that this extends psychoanalytic thinking, in that it creates a third object between mouth and breast in a way that not only separates them but also creates a potential space for their reunion. It implies the idea of something that is not present, which is another meaning of the negative. Thus Winnicott explored the notion of the negative without it ever acquiring the status of a concept in his work.

Some aspects of these patients who function in the negative, Green suggests, could, however, not have been understood by Winnicott because of his lack of attention to the drives.

If such patients seem so vulnerable, on the one hand, they also express an impossibility to change, as they function under the register of the repetition compulsion. This is what Green has referred to as *primary anality* (1993), emphasising the narcissistic aspects of the fixation. This is characterised by an "*unconscious negativism where it is more important to say no to the object than yes to oneself*" (Green, 1999a, p. 286, italics in original). According to Green, Winnicott did not pay sufficient attention to this phenomenon, as they belonged to the register of drives whose role Winnicott underestimated, when he focused his thinking on the objects and the space.

Bion's contribution to the understanding of the work of the negative may be identified in several of his concepts, particularly his distinction between no-thing and nothing; thoughts without thinker and thinking as needing thoughts to be thought by a thinker (thinking apparatus) (Green, 1997).

The primordial mind is made of beta-elements, the domain of thoughts that have no thinker (Bion, 1992, p. 313). Beta-elements belong to the sensorial domain. The transformation of beta-elements into alpha-elements requires the existence of an object that is capable of reverie. The process of having thoughts with a thinker implies the transformation of beta-elements into alpha-elements. Bion suggests that this becomes possible in the relationship between infant and mother when normal projective identification is enabled and precludes the development of an alpha-function and therefore a differentiation of elements into conscious and unconscious.

What happens if the object is absent for too long? For Klein, the absence of the object is linked to persecutory anxiety and a bad object that is installed. For Bion, the lack of transformation of beta-elements into alpha-elements does not mean that a bad object is there instead. The individual struggles with "nameless dread". He states:

> Normal development follows if the relationship between infant and breast permits the infant to project a feeling, say, that it is dying into the mother and to reintroject it after its sojourn in the breast has made it tolerable to the infant psyche. If the projection is not accepted by the mother the infant feels that its feeling that it is dying is *stripped of such meaning* as it has. It therefore reintrojects, not a fear of dying made tolerable, but a nameless dread. [Bion, 1962, p. 116, italics added]

Levine, Reed, and Scarfone (2013) have pointed out a link between Freud's notion of the drive and Bion's (1962, 1970) concept of beta-elements as proto-psychic forms not suitable to be thought about. According to Levine and colleagues, similarly to Freud's notion of the drive, beta-elements "made an implicit demand ('turbulence') upon the psyche for work (alpha-function)" (Levine, Reed, & Scarfone, 2013, p. 5). They refer to Green's (1986a, 2005a) notion of "a tear in the fabric of the psyche", a failure in the capacity to represent. Scarfone also draws a parallel between Freud's "quota of affect" and Bion's beta-elements (Levine, Reed, & Scarfone 2013, p. 89). Sebastian Kohon (2014) has recently suggested similarities between the concept of "drive" and Bion's beta-element, thus emphasising the "economic" aspect present in Bion's formulations.[4]

Green believes that a part of beta-elements, which can only be expelled, remain permanently in the mind in a state of exclusion (Green, 1998, p. 654).

Green also explores Bion's ideas on "O", "K", and "–K", as well as Bion's reference to Keats's negative capability. If K symbolises knowledge, –K symbolises active ignorance, an avoidance of awareness and truth. Particularly relevant is the idea of "negative knowledge" and the distinction between *non-understanding* and *misunderstanding*. The latter puts an end to the process of understanding.

One is referring to the distinction between the *absence* of the breast and the *annihilation* of the breast. Green's writing is here evocative and powerful. The evacuation of thoughts leads to a blank state or a hole in the psyche.

Green's contribution to a theory of thinking lies in the articulation of his study of the negative in relation to thirdness. As I discuss in chapter 2, he insists on the constitutive structure of the negative hallucination. The mother leaves the impression of her arms on the child, which constitutes the framing structure that, in her absence, contains the loss of the perception of the maternal object, as a negative hallucination of it. Green believes that it is against the background of negativity that future representations of the object are inscribed. This is the beginning of psychic life, the outcome of the work of mourning of the primordial object. Phantasy life takes place in the absence of the object—ideas that will have important implications for an understanding of clinical facts and cultural life.[5] In terms of a theory of technique, this emphasises the relevance of the silence as well as the absence of the analyst as it is in this empty space that phantasy life and representations emerge, as in the dream screen, "defined as the blank background upon which the dream picture appears to be projected" (Lewin, 1948, p. 224).

The dimension that separates Green from both Winnicott and Bion and brings him back towards Freud is the relevance of the mother's body, and therefore of sexuality. Green's conceptualisation of the mother of the "framing structure" is also the erotic mother—the mother that, Freud argues in *An Outline of Psycho-Analysis* (1940a [1938]), is the first seductress of the infant through the care that she gives him and her general attitude in relation to him. In this way Green also distinguishes between his conceptualisation of the framing structure and Winnicott's concept of holding.

La pensée clinique

All the concepts developed by Green throughout his extensive work come together in terms of his model for clinical thought.

For Green, the therapeutic encounter takes place over many layers. The patient tells a story: of his origins, of his family or parents.

The analyst is silent, paying receptive, suspended attention, facing the patient's free associations. In the current situation, the patient's past conflictual knots may have been reactivated: affects, sexual life, professional life, social relationships. All these aspects make an indissociable whole, like a piece of music in which the analyst may pick up the themes and variations and outline the contours of the Oedipus of childhood or an infantile neurosis. On his part, the patient has an expectation of how the analytic process will work, on the one hand, whereas at the same time, on the other hand, there are areas linked to his narcissism or masochism that he does not want to change.

Green points out the traditional categories for assessment of analysability, such as whether one is dealing with a neurotic or non-neurotic structure, and the ego's weakness or strength. He suggests that nowadays one tends to analyse the patient's analysability—a hypothetical evaluation that is predictive. The question at stake is the "capacity of being alone in the presence of the analyst". Through this artificial state of solitude, the patient is invited to enter a state of mental functioning similar to dreaming.

Green believes that the specificity of psychoanalytic practice is inaugurated with Dora's analysis (Freud, 1905e [1901]), followed by the other four major clinical cases: Little Hans (1909b), the Rat Man (1909d), Schreber (1911c [1910]), and the Wolf Man (1918b [1914]). Together they inaugurate the specific psychoanalytic presentation of a clinical case (Green, 2002c). Key psychoanalytic concepts, such as infantile sexuality, unconscious phantasy, the Oedipus complex, are understood through the lens of the transference. The analytic setting is initiated. Green progressively elaborates other aspects of the setting, including the double transference—namely, transference onto speech and transference onto the object (Green, 1983), countertransference, the psychoanalytic third, and the heterogeneity of the signifier. Since Freud, the role of the object has been emphasised more, although Green believes that this at times tend to be over-emphasised at the expense of leaving aside the fundamental role of the drives. The specificity of the analytic clinical thought, however, requires the relationship between the intrapsychic and the intersubjective. Otherwise major types of psychopathologies, such as those we have been discussing in this Introduction, would be incomprehensible.

The setting as the analytic third

Green characterises the analytic situation as psychoanalytic association. The setting only has value as a metaphor for another concept (such as dreams, the incest taboo, parricide, maternal care, etc.).

Bleger (1967) and Winnicott (1971b), each in his own framework, recognised the existence of the setting as a transitional state between symbiosis (Bleger) and potential reunion (Winnicott). According to Green, the setting contains a triangular paradigm uniting three polarities: *dreams* (narcissism), *maternal care* (of the mother, according to Winnicott), and the *prohibition of incest* (of the father, according to Freud). The symbolisation of the setting is therefore the symbolisation of the unconscious structure of the Oedipus complex, which is elicited by the setting.

Green's notion of heterochrony and his exploration of Freud's notions of the phylogenesis and ontogenesis in the constitution of the unconscious phantasies are crucial to understand this metaphoric dimension of the setting. Temporality is not derived from the individual experiences alone but is to be understood in the intersection between the individual and the cultural.

The topographical model developed the centrality of the role of sexuality: the first sexual experiences take place in the intersection between the internal and the external, expressed initially by the maternal care. The analysis of Little Hans (Freud, 1909b) brings forth the dimension of parental discourse. Childhood sexuality meets the discourse of the parent's own sexuality. Freud was concerned with the individual's prehistory, with the unconscious theories that children give to the mysteries of sexuality—their own and their parents'—that are related to the questions about their origins. Freud then turns to other societies in his anthropological writings in search of what Lacan termed key signifiers. The myth of the murder of the father (Freud, 1912–13), with the corollaries of incestuous desire and parricidal wishes, offered a psychoanalytic interpretation to the origins of culture (Green, 2007a, p. 10).

In *Totem and Taboo* (1912–13), where genetic inheritance is emphasised, Freud also suggests another dimension of transmission that can be understood in terms of what Green has called the "the *disposition to re-acquisition*". Primal fantasies are re-actualised through individual experience (Green, 2007a, p. 13). Consider the following passage: The inheritance of psychic dispositions *"needs to be given some sort of impetus in the life of the individual before they can be roused into actual operation"* (Freud, 1912–13, p. 15, emphasis added). This sounds like what Bion would refer to as preconceptions awaiting realisation. In this formulation, the role of the object becomes crucial. Later, Freud also added:

> Everyone possesses in his unconscious mental activity an apparatus which enables him to interpret other people's reactions, that is, to undo the distortions which other people have imposed on the expression of their feelings. An unconscious understanding such as this of all the customs, ceremonies and dogmas left behind by the original relation to the father may have made it possible for later generations to take over their heritage of emotion. [Freud, 1912–13, p. 159]

This is at the basis of the truly psychoanalytic approach to the question of unconscious transmission: what is transmitted from adult to child, from mother to baby, is done unconsciously. Unconscious phantasies, primary repression, and primary identification (with both parents) suggest that the infant is born into a triangular structure that precedes him, and it is in the context of that structure that he will form his identifications. The concept of the superego introduced in 1923 (Freud, 1923b) offers the key to the questions of transmission. The structural model of the mind underlines both the biological heredity of the id and the cultural determinance of the superego.

According to Green, the analytic setting offers a context in which these dramas are actualised in the present.

> Two contradictory moments in time, one archaic and the other possessing the acquisitions of history, share between them the maternal bodily psychic space; and there is nothing to decide in favour of one or the other. My hypothesis of heterochrony is thus situated here on a strictly ontogenic level, which can be detected in the synchrony of the present, without any reference of the mnemic traces left by the species. [Green, 2007a, p. 20]

The fundamental psychoanalytic rule, Green suggests, inscribes a third as a law under the two parties. The aim of the psychoanalytic process is not so much to make something conscious, as to recognise the unconscious. All this takes place within a conception of psychoanalysis that recognises the existence of clinical thought (Green, 2002c).

The central phobic position: associative avoidance and the heterogeneity of the signifier

Green's paper on the central phobic position (Green, 2000a) has already become a classic, and it is perhaps an example of what he describes above. It is interesting that some parts of the paper are still couched in the language of Freud's "Project" (1950 [1895]), perhaps with the aim of indicating that the relevance of the metapsychology had already been announced in that work. The paper is a reflection on free associations and the type of communication established in the session of a borderline patient (Green, 2000a).

Green identifies a particular form of associative behaviour that enables such patients to maintain a central defensive position and a particular phobic functioning of the mind—a defence against anal penetration or against the fear of losing one's boundaries. In his example—one of the few that Green presented at greater length—the patient's discourse seemed to have the function of keeping both patient and analyst at a distance from each other. What was present was not a lack but, rather, an excess of associations.

Green came to understand that such defence does not have the aim of preventing a single trauma to emerge to consciousness: rather, one is dealing with the internal relations between the different traumatic constellations (2000a, p. 435). The patient presents an *associative avoidance* rather than attacks on linking; he reveals a state of threat caused by the consequence of establishing meaningful links between a number of themes in the patient's mind. These themes are threatening not only for the sanctions of the superego but also for the ego's organisation, and therefore the fear of becoming mad.

Green suggests the notion of the "heterogeneity of the signifier" (1999b). A patient's communication is expressed through various channels of significations—representation, affect, bodily states, acting-out behaviour—which, combined, enable the analyst to reach the *dynamic picture* of what is communicated (2000a, p. 443). This understanding also situates the patient's discourse in time, in terms of *après-coup*. One is dealing not with a linear sequence but with a complex set of interactions that include a before and after: "retroactive reverberation and heralding anticipation" (p. 444). Green is here expressing his views on analytic temporality.[6]

Transference

Green points to the shift in Freud's thinking in *Beyond the Pleasure Principle* (1920g). From this work on, transference is not only in the service of pleasure, but also concerns the repetition of unpleasure. The change from the topographical model of the mind to the structural model indicates the shift from a movement based on desire to a model of discharge of the drives into action. The analyst now faces not only the unconscious desires, but also the drives themselves.

Green suggests that in certain schools of thought, where the analysis is restricted to the interpretation of the transference, there is a limitation of the analytic task that is prejudicial to the freedom and spontaneity of discourse and represents a return to suggestion. He believes that the British school is centred on the interpretation of the transference, whereas the French school establishes the distinction between interpretation *dans le transfert* (in the transference) and interpretation *de transfert* (transference interpretation; see Donnet, 2001). He believes that all interpretations take place within the transference context (*le cadre du transfert*), even when they do not allude to it. All the material in any analysis contains elements belonging to different temporal dimensions. Green's views of the work that is undertaken in England seem to me not to be representative of the full range of thinking among British analysts. The issues of interpretation in the transference only versus the role of extra-transference interpretations, as well as interpretations in the here and now only versus reconstructions, are, indeed, sources of heated debate among British analysts.

Countertransference

Green reviews the history of the development of the concept of countertransference, starting with Paula Heimann, who in 1950 viewed it as the result of an unconscious wish of the patient to communicate to the analyst the affects that he experienced but could not verbalise.

> When traumas occur before language is acquired, remembering is impossible . . . the transference is then a process of actualization more than one of remembering, for the analysand does not recognise the return of the past in it. . . . I propose to call this phenomenon *amnesic remembering outside the field of conscious and unconscious memories.* [Green, 2002d, p. 89, emphasis in original]

Green traces the development of the concept among the inter-subjectivists in America and in France. French analysts' work with the countertransference refers to a different field of conceptualisation than that of the British analysts. One of their main influences is Kristeva and her concept of *chora*: the maternal receptacle necessary for the reception of impressions, sensations, and affects crucial to the elaboration of the symbolic function. The *chora* is an "ancient, mobile, unstable receptacle, prior to the One, to the Father, and even to the syllable" (Kristeva, 1987, p. 5). It precedes the establishment of the linguistic sign and manifests itself as a space where the subject is both generated and negated. It is a subversive space where the subject is threatened with annihilation and simultaneously produced (Kristeva, 1984).

In the analytic process the analyst is confronted by the fundamental experience of distress [*Hilflosigkeit*] in the patient. The analyst's countertransference is receptive to the traces left by these infantile experiences. By inviting the patient to abandon the control mechanisms, the analytic situation may revive the traumatic situation.

The intrapsychic and the intersubjective

Green emphasised the indissoluble link between drives and objects. The construction of the object leads retrospectively to the hypothesis of the drive, which reciprocally constructs the object. Force and meaning are intertwined and combine their effects.

If the analysis of the patient's internal world is the main focus of contemporary analytic work, the way in which the analyst has access to this process is through the analysis of that which is projected by the patient. It is from the matrix of the transference and countertransference, as discussed above, that meaning is reached. This is the domain of the interpersonal, although Green is very clear about how he conceptualises this, in a way that is different from the American intersubjective school.

This leads to his concept of the double limit: the horizontal limit is that between consciousness on the upper level and the unconscious on the lower level. Two fields were thus defined: that of the intrapsychic on the inside, and that of the intersubjective—that is, the distinction between inside and outside, which requires a relationship to the other.

> For where psychic structuring is concerned, the outside is not only reality, but at its heart, symbolizing it and signifying it, that which psychoanalysis denotes as the object—which in fact refers to the other subject. The object is thus situated in two places: it belongs both to the internal space on the two levels of the conscious and the unconscious, and it is also present in the external space as object, as other, as another subject. [Green, 2000b, p. 3]

The object is also multiple, Green states, in contrast to British psychoanalysis, which is centred on the primary object, the mother or her breast, making all the varieties of the primitive world derive from this initial model. By contrast, he suggests that French psychoanalytic literature emphasises structural distinctions that cannot be absorbed by a developmental genetic position.

Green returns to the *New Introductory Lectures on Psycho-Analysis*: ". . . on its path from its source to its aim the instinct becomes operative psychically" (Freud, 1933a, p. 96).

Freud conceived of the drive as anchored in the body. However, the closer the drive came to its aim—that is, of course, to the object—the more it became "psychically operative". The crucial dimension of the drive is the idea of *forces* capable of evolution yet maintaining a greater or lesser irreducible portion of their original state.

> A corollary may be added to this: what allows us to get away from the exclusive domination of force is *representation*, which acquires the power to present itself as a substitute object for the object of the drive. Thanks to representation, force is displaced; it is used advantageously to hold together the elements of representation and to fix them, relatively speaking—thus allowing their transformation. [Green, 2000b, pp. 30–31]

This force acquires psychic meaning through representation. Yet it can never be fully represented. It represents something that is, by definition, always in excess.

To quote from a previous paper of mine (Perelberg, 2003; see also Perelberg, 2015b):

> . . . I have pointed to "the modernity of the concept of *pulsion*", as a concept-limit that is still powerful and relevant, in that it refers to that which is at the limit of conceptualisation. A substantial part of psychic phenomena remains opaque and seems to escape all causalities (Green, 1998, 2000a). This implies a view of the mind that is not unitary, either in terms of content or structure. The concept of "border" pushes for the notion of "movement", of something that always lies beyond full understanding. It reintroduces Freud's notion of a disjunction between drives and phantasies. The theory of "drives" is the theoretical support for the presence of a force in psychic life, which resists both evolution and taming [Perelberg, 2003, p. 590]

Death drives[7]

Freud continuously modified his views on the aggressive or destructive instincts. In his initial theoretical formulation (Freud, 1905e [1901]), the aggressive impulses were considered to be

derivatives of a drive for sexual mastery. This view was not modified for some ten years. In "Instincts and Their Vicissitudes"
(1915c), Freud traced the origins of the instincts to sources of
stimulation within the organism. His central thesis was that "the
true prototypes of the relation of hate are derived not from sexual life, but from the ego's struggle to preserve and maintain
itself" (p. 138). One of the vicissitudes of sexual instincts is the
reversal into its opposite, love being transformed into hate. At
that point Freud postulated that the drive for mastery, in conjunction with other drives, served self-preservation and was part
of the self-preservative instinct.

Further elaboration in Freud's formulations stems from both
conceptual and clinical developments. Freud had identified the role
of aggression in his clinical work and in his conceptual framework,
such as his formulations on the Oedipus complex, as seen already
in *The Interpretation of Dreams* (1900a; see also Laplanche & Pontalis,
1985). The main theoretical problem Freud faced, however, was
how to reconcile an impulse that leads to self-destruction or to the
destruction of the other with the frame of reference that postulated
the duality of libido and self-preservative instincts.

It was with *Beyond the Pleasure Principle* (1920g) and the discussion of the death instinct that Freud allowed for the emergence
of an autonomous aggressive drive [*Aggressionstrieb*]. Aggression
against the external world represents an externalisation of the
death instinct, with the help of the muscular apparatus. This non-
sexual aggressive drive is present from the beginning of life and
works continually to unbind connections, in contrast with Eros,
which seeks to bind. He stated, in 1937:

> If we take into consideration the total picture made up of
> phenomena of masochism immanent in so many people, the
> negative therapeutic reaction and the sense of guilt found in
> so many neurotics, we shall no longer be able to adhere to the
> belief that mental events are exclusively governed by the desire
> for pleasure. These phenomena are unmistakable indications of
> the presence of a power in mental life which we call the instinct
> of aggression or of destruction according to its aims, and which
> we trace back to the original death instinct of living matter.
> [Freud, 1937c, p. 243]

Psychoanalysts have tended to equate the opposition between the life and death instincts with that between sexuality and aggressiveness. As Freud himself did not develop the concept of aggression in the same way as he developed that of libido, psychoanalysts have tended to trace parallels between libido and aggression. The concept of the death instinct, however, contains several related ideas that are connected not only with aggression, but also with passivity, as in the Nirvana principle, and the repetition compulsion, which has no special affinity with aggressive behaviour (Laplanche & Pontalis, 1985).

In *An Outline of Psycho-Analysis*, Freud postulated two basic instincts: Eros and the destructive instinct.

> The aim of the first of these basic instincts is to establish ever greater units and to preserve them thus—in short, to bind together; the aim of the second is, on the contrary, to undo connections and to destroy things. In the case of the destructive instinct we may suppose that its final aim is to lead what is living into inorganic state. [Freud, 1940a [1938], p. 148]

The notion of binding and unbinding is central here. It is in connection with these two mechanisms that Green introduces the notions of *objectalising and disobjectalising functions* (Green, 2007b). The first means not only the relationship to an object, but the capacity to transform structures into an object "even when the object is no longer directly invoked" (Green, 1999c, p. 85).

In contrast, the disobjectalising function is decathexis, the withdrawal of investment.

Green points out that the death drive is a *concept*, and no clinical presentation can be evidence of its existence, especially as any phenomenon can give rise to multiple interpretations.

The introduction of the concept of the death drives implies a review of the whole of Freud's theoretical formulations. Now narcissism can be thought of as in the service of the libidinal investment of the self, as in the 1914 text (1914c); it is the core of the life instincts (Green, 2007b, p. 53). Green differentiates between a life narcissism and death narcissism (above). The latter expresses the tendency to reach a zero level of excitation, in the service of the disobjectalising function, linked to the death drive. It is present in the psychoses.

In *Beyond the Pleasure Principle,* after introducing the death instinct, Freud states that "there might be such a thing as primary masochism" (1920g, p. 22), which finds its development in "The Economic Problem of Masochism" (1924c). In this paper he grappled with what he called the "enigma of masochism". He asked himself whether pain and displeasure could become a goal of mental life. If that happens, then what becomes of the pleasure principle?

Freud's suggestion is that a portion of the death instinct remains in the organism, and becomes libidinally bound there. It is this portion that Freud indicates has been recognised as the original erotogenic masochism (1924c, p. 164). This primary erotogenic masochism is directed towards the subject himself and is the expression of the fusion of the death instinct with the libidinal drives: "even the subject's destruction of himself cannot take place without libidinal satisfaction" (p. 170).

Green considers that Freud's ideas on the death drive find an axis in his anthropological works, culminating in his *Civilization and Its Discontents* (1930a), three years before the ascent of Nazism. It is in the cultural domain that the death instinct finds its most destructive aspects. The concept of the superego provided a link between the work of the negative in the individual and the cultural domains.

Green reflects further on the role of the negative in culture in the final chapter of *Illusions and Disillusions of Psychoanalytic Work* (2011a). He discovers the work of Imre Kertész (*The Holocaust as Culture*, 2012) and Vasili Grossman (*Everything Flows*, 2009). Both these writings touch him deeply. *Everything Flows* is the last novel that Grossman wrote. The main narrative follows the struggle of a 50-year-old man in post-Stalinist Russia who is released after having spent 30 years of his life in the Gulag. He encounters a process of destalinisation in the Soviet Union, where everything is experienced by him as a lie, where statements falsify reality and truth (Green, 2011a, p. 186).

Kertész, in an essay entitled *Holocaust as Culture* (2012), considers Auschwitz, not as the name of a camp, but of an epoch; it is the most important event since the Cross. It is the rupture of contract as a motor of power. The achievement of totalitarianism was to have placed man outside the law. This leads Green to pose the question (see also Perelberg, 2015a):

> should we think conceptually about the negative in two distinct forms which homogeneity alone can unite but which involve two radically separate significations one which opposes the negative as psychoanalysis allows us to envisage it, and the other which is derived from socio-political thinking as we find it developed at length by Kertész? [Green, 2011a, p. 181]

Green concludes by suggesting two types of negative that can be contrasted in terms of unconscious masochism and perversion. The first turns against itself, the other is externalised and tries to impose itself: "melancholia leads psychic life, but delusional perversion seeks to take possession at all costs of all the forms of power" (Green, 2011a, p. 186). He believes it is the task of the psychoanalyst to fight against both forms in the name of truth.

Notes

1. I would like to refer to some of the excellent articles and books on the work of André Green—namely, Duparc (1996), Kohon (1999a, 1999b), Parsons (1996), Pirlot & Cupa (2012), Urribarri (2013), Reed, Levine, & Scarfone (2013), and Delourmel (2013). This Introduction is organised around key concepts that Green has elaborated in the course of his life, including his later work, and that have influenced my thinking.

2. In England several authors have considered the notion of space in their formulations about the analytic process: Balint (1959), with his contrast between ocnophile patients, who experience objects as safe but the space between them and their objects as unsafe, and philobats, for whom the objects are hostile and therefore the space between them is experienced as safe; Glasser (1979), with his notion of the "core complex" in perversions; Britton (2003), with narcissistic detachment and narcissistic adherence; and Perelberg (2003, 2004, 2015a), with the distinction between patients who create full or empty spaces in the analyst's mind.

3. Most of what follows in this section is derived from Perelberg, 1995.

4. Green nevertheless indicates that while "for Freud the drives always had their source in the most inner part of the body . . . for Bion, beta-elements may also arise from external stimuli in the primordial mind" (Green, 1998, p. 653). A discussion of the differentiation between Freud's concept of the drives and Bion's beta-elements may be found also in Perelberg 2015b.

5. An analysis of the way in which the role of the negative is central in the understanding of the aesthetics experience is explored by Kohon (2016;

see also chapter 4, this volume). The author reflects on how creativity may be expressed through negativity and incompleteness, a process that points out to the "commonality of experience" between the aesthetics and psychoanalysis.

6. I have suggested that time is an essential element in establishing third-ness, creating a link between the here and now and the there and then in the *après coup* of the psychoanalytic process (Perelberg, 2013).

7. This section is a combination of two previous publications, Perelberg (1999, pp. 20–21) and Perelberg (2015a, pp. 176–177).

References

Balint, M. (1959). *Thrills and Regression*. Madison, CT: International Universities Press.

Balint, M. (1968). *The Basic Fault: Therapeutic Aspects of Regression*. London: Tavistock Publications.

Bion, W. R. (1957). Differentiation of the psychotic from the non-psychotic personalities. In: *Second Thoughts*. London: Heinemann, 1967; reprinted London: Karnac, 1984.

Bion, W. R. (1959). Attacks on linking. In: *Second Thoughts*. London: Heinemann, 1967; reprinted London: Karnac, 1984.

Bion, W. R. (1962). A theory of thinking. In: *Second Thoughts* (pp. 110–119). London: Heinemann, 1967; reprinted London: Karnac, 1984. [First published as: The psycho-analytic study of thinking. *International Journal of Psychoanalysis, 43*: 306–310.]

Bion, W. R. (1970). *Attention and Interpretation*. London: Tavistock Publications; reprinted London: Karnac, 1984.

Bion, W. R. (1992). *Cogitations*. London: Karnac; new extended edition, 1994.

Bleger, J. (1967). Psycho-analysis of the psycho-analytic frame. *International Journal of Psychoanalysis, 48*: 511–519.

Bouvet, M. (1956). La Clinique psychanalytique. La Relation d'objet. In: *Oeuvres Psychanalytique, I. La Relation d'objet*. Paris: Payot, 1967.

Bouvet, M. (1958). Technical variations and the concept of distance. *International Journal of Psychoanalysis, 39*: 211–221.

Braunschweig, D., & Fain, M. (1975). *La Nuit, le jour: Essai psychanalytique sur le fonctionnement mental*. Paris: Presses Universitaires de France.

Britton, R. (2003). Narcissistic problems in sharing space. In: *Sex, Death and the Superego* (pp. 164–178). London: Karnac.

Delourmel, C. (2013). An introduction to the work of André Green. *International Journal of Psychoanalysis, 94*: 133–156.

Deutsch, H. (1942). Some forms of emotional disturbance and their relationship to schizophrenia. *Psychoanalytic Quarterly, 11*: 301–321.

Donnet, J.-L. (2001). From the fundamental rule to the analysing situation. *International Journal of Psychoanalysis, 82*: 129–140.

Donnet, J.-L., & Green, A. (1973). *L'Enfant de ça. Psychanalyse d'un entretien. La psychose blanche.* Paris: Éditions de Minuit.

Duparc, F. (1996). *André Green.* Paris: Presses Universitaires de France.

Erikson, E. H. (1959). *Identity and the Life Cycle.* New York: International Universities Press.

Fain, M. (1966). Regression et psychosomatique. *Revue Française de Psychanalyse, 30*: 451–456.

Fairbairn, W. R. D. (1940). Schizoid factors in the personality. In: *Psychoanalytic Studies of the Personality.* London: Tavistock Publications, 1952.

Freud, S. (1900a). *The Interpretation of Dreams. Standard Edition, 4–5.*

Freud, S. (1901a). *On Dreams. Standard Edition, 5*: 629–714.

Freud, S. (1905e [1901]). Fragment of an analysis of a case of hysteria. *Standard Edition, 7*: 1–122.

Freud, S. (1909b). Analysis of a phobia in a five-year-old boy. *Standard Edition, 9*: 1–150.

Freud, S. (1909d). Notes upon a case of obsessional neurosis. *Standard Edition, 10*: 153–318.

Freud, S. (1911c [1910]). Psycho-analytic notes on an autobiographical account of a case of paranoia. *Standard Edition, 12*: 3–82.

Freud, S. (1912–13). *Totem and Taboo. Standard Edition, 13*: 1–255.

Freud, S. (1914c). On narcissism. *Standard Edition, 14*: 73–104.

Freud, S. (1915c). Instincts and their vicissitudes. *Standard Edition, 14*: 109–140.

Freud, S. (1915d). Repression. *Standard Edition, 14*: 141–158.

Freud, S. (1915e). The unconscious. *Standard Edition, 14*: 159–216.

Freud, S. (1917d [1915]). A metapsychological supplement to the theory of dreams. *Standard Edition, 14*: 217–235.

Freud, S. (1917e [1915]). Mourning and melancholia. *Standard Edition, 14*: 237–258.

Freud, S. (1918b [1914]). From the history of an infantile neurosis. *Standard Edition, 17*: 3–123.

Freud, S. (1920g). *Beyond the Pleasure Principle. Standard Edition, 18*: 7–64.

Freud, S. (1923b). *The Ego and the Id. Standard Edition, 19*: 12–66.

Freud, S. (1924c). The economic problem of masochism. *Standard Edition, 19*: 159–170.

Freud, S. (1925h). Negation. *Standard Edition, 19*: 235–240.

Freud, S. (1926d [1925]). *Inhibitions, Symptoms and Anxiety. Standard Edition, 20*: 77–175.

Freud, S. (1930a). *Civilization and Its Discontents. Standard Edition, 21*: 57–146.

Freud, S. (1933a). *New Introductory Lectures on Psycho-Analysis. Standard Edition, 22*: 3–182.

Freud, S. (1937c). Analysis terminable and interminable. *Standard Edition, 23*: 209–254.

Freud, S. (1937d). Constructions in analysis. *Standard Edition, 23*: 255–269.

Freud, S. (1940a [1938]). *An Outline of Psycho-Analysis. Standard Edition, 23*: 139–208.

Freud, S.(1950 [1892–1899]). Extracts from the Fliess Papers. *Standard Edition, 1*: 173–280.

Freud, S. (1950 [1895]). Project for a scientific psychology. *Standard Edition, 1*: 281–391.

Gitelson, M. (1958). On ego distortions [Panel discussion]. *International Journal of Psychoanalysis, 50*: 245–256.

Glasser, M. (1979). Some aspects of the role of aggression in the perversions. In: I. Rosen. (Ed.), *Sexual Deviation*. Oxford: Oxford University Press.

Green, A. (1973). *Le Discours vivant*. Paris: Presses Universitaires de France.

Green, A. (1975). The analyst, symbolization and absence in the analytic setting (On changes in analytic practice and analytic experience)—In Memory of D. W. Winnicott. *International Journal of Psychoanalysis, 56*: 1–22.

Green, A. (1977). Conceptions of affect. *International Journal of Psychoanalysis, 58*: 129–156. Also in *On Private Madness* (pp. 174–213). London: Hogarth Press & The Institute of Psychoanalysis, 1986.

Green, A. (1983). *Le Langage dans la psychanalyse*. In: *Langages rencontres Psychanalytiques d'Aix-en-Provence 1983* (pp. 179–206). Paris: Les Belles Lettres, 1984.

Green, A. (1986a). The analyst, symbolization and absence in the analytic setting. In: *On Private Madness* (pp. 30–59). London: Hogarth Press & The Institute of Psychoanalysis.

Green, A. (1986b). The borderline concept. In: *On Private Madness* (pp. 60–83). London: Hogarth Press & The Institute of Psychoanalysis.

Green, A. (1986c). The dead mother. In: *On Private Madness* (pp. 142–173). London: Hogarth Press & The Institute of Psychoanalysis.

Green, A. (1986d). Passions and their vicissitudes. In: *On Private Madness* (pp. 214–253). London: Hogarth Press & The Institute of Psychoanalysis.

Green, A. (1986e). Potential space in psychoanalysis. In: *On Private Madness* (pp. 277–296). London: Hogarth Press & The Institute of Psychoanalysis.

Green, A. (1986f). *On Private Madness.* London: Hogarth Press & The Institute of Psychoanalysis.

Green, A. (1986g). Psychoanalysis and ordinary modes of thought. In: *On Private Madness* (pp. 17–29). London: Hogarth Press & The Institute of Psychoanalysis.

Green, A. (1992). *La Déliaison.* Paris: Les Belles Lettres.

Green, A. (1993). L'Analité primaire dans la relation anale. In: *La Névrose* obsessionnelle (pp. 61–86). Paris: Presses Universitaires de France.

Green, A. (1995). *Propédeutique. La Métapsychologie revisitée.* Seyssel: Champ Vallon.

Green, A. (1997). The intuition of the negative in "Playing and Reality". *International Journal of Psychoanalysis, 78* (6): 1071–1084.

Green, A. (1998). The primordial mind and the work of the negative. *International Journal of Psychoanalysis, 79*: 649–665.

Green, A. (1999a). Appendices. In: *The Work of the Negative* (pp. 269–291). London: Free Association Books.

Green, A. (1999b). *The Fabric of Affect and Psychoanalytic Discourse.* London: Routledge.

Green, A. (1999c). *The Work of the Negative.* London: Free Association Books.

Green, A. (2000a). The central phobic position. *International Journal of Psychoanalysis, 81*: 429–451.

Green, A. (2000b). The intrapsychic and intersubjective in psychoanalysis. *Psychoanalytic Quarterly., 69*: 1–39.

Green, A. (2001). *Life Narcissism, Death Narcissism.* London: Free Association Books.

Green, A. (2002a). A dual conception of narcissism. *Psychoanalytic Quarterly, 71*: 631–649.

Green, A. (2002b). *Idées directrices pour une psychanalyse contemporaine.* Paris: Presses Universitaires de France.

Green, A. (2002c). *La Pensée clinique.* Paris: Odile Jacob.

Green, A. (2002d). *Time in Psychoanalysis: Some Contradictory Aspects,* trans. A. Weller. London: Free Association Books.

Green, A. (2003). *Diachrony in Psychoanalysis,* trans. A. Weller. London: Free Association Books.

Green, A. (2004). Thirdness and psychoanalytic concepts. *Psychoanalytic Quarterly, 73*: 99–135.

Green, A. (2005a). *Key Ideas for a Contemporary Psychoanalysis: Misrecognition and Recognition of the Unconscious,* trans. A. Weller. London: Routledge.

Green, A. (2005b). Negation. In: R. J. Perelberg (Ed.), *Freud: A Modern Reader* (pp. 253–273). London: Whurr.

Green, A. (2005c). *Psychoanalysis: A Paradigm for Clinical Thinking,* trans. A. Weller. London: Free Association Books.

Green, A. (2007a). The construction of heterochrony (pp. 1–22). In: R. J. Perelberg (Ed.), *Time and Memory*: London: Karnac.

Green, A. (2007b). *Pourquoi les pulsions de destruction ou de mort?* Paris: Éditions du Panama.

Green, A. (2011a). *Illusions and Disillusions of Psychoanalytic Work.* London: Karnac.

Green, A. (2011b). Les Cas limite. De La Folie privée aux pulsions de destruction et de mort. *Revue Française de Psychanalyse, 75*: 375–390.

Grossman, V. (2009). *Everything Flows.* New York: New York Review of Books.

Heimann, P. (1950). On counter-transference. *International Journal of Psychoanalysis, 31*: 81–84.

Kernberg, O. F. (1970). A psychoanalytic classification of character pathology. *Journal of the American Psychoanalytic Association, 18*: 800–822.

Kernberg, O. F. (1974). Contrasting viewpoints regarding the nature and psychoanalytic treatment of narcissistic personalities. *Journal of the American Psychoanalytic Association, 22* (2): 255–267.

Kertész, I. (2012). *The Holocaust as Culture*, trans. T. Cooper. Calcutta: Seagull Books.

Klein, M. (1946). Notes on some schizoid mechanisms. In: M. Klein, P. Heimann, S. Isaacs, & J. Riviere, *Developments in Psycho-Analysis*. London: Hogarth Press, 1952; reprinted London: Karnac, 1989.

Kohon, G. (1999a). The Greening of psychoanalysis: André Green in dialogues with Gregorio Kohon. In: G. Kohon (Ed.), *The Dead Mother: The Work of André Green* (pp. 10–58). London: Routledge.

Kohon, G. (1999b). Introduction. In: G. Kohon (Ed.), *The Dead Mother: The Work of André Green* (pp. 1–10). London: Routledge.

Kohon, G. (2005). Love in a time of madness. In: A. Green & G. Kohon, *Love and Its Vicissitudes* (pp. 41–100). London: Karnac.

Kohon, G. (2007). Borderline traces and the question of diagnoses. In: A. Green (Ed.), *Resonance of Suffering: Countertransference in Non-Neurotic Structures*. London: Karnac.

Kohon, G. (2016). *Reflections on the Aesthetic Experience: Psychoanalysis and the Uncanny*. London: Routledge.

Kohon, S. (2014). Making contact with the primitive mind: The contact-barrier, beta-elements and the drives. *International Journal of Psychoanalysis, 95* (2): 245–270.

Kohut, H. (1971). *The Analysis of the Self*. New York: International Universities Press.

Kristeva, J. (1984). *Revolution in Poetic Language*. New York: Columbia University Press.

Kristeva, J. (1987). *Tales of Love*, trans. L. Roudiez. New York: Columbia University Press.

Lacan, J. (2005). *Des Noms-du-père*. Paris: Éditions du Seuil.

Laplanche, J., & Pontalis, J.-B. (1985). *Fantasme originaire. Fantasme des origins. Origines du fantasme*. Paris: Hachette.

Levine, H. B., Reed, G. B., & Scarfone, D. (Eds.) (2013). *Unrepresented States and the Construction of Meaning*. London: Karnac.

Lewin, B. D. (1948). Inferences from the dream screen. *International Journal of Psychoanalysis, 29*: 224–231.

Mannoni, O. (1968). *Freud*. Paris: Éditions du Seuil.

Marty, P., M'Uzan, M. de, & David, C. (1963). *L'Investigation psychosomatique. Sept observations cliniques*. Paris: Presses Universitaires de France.

McDougall, J. (1972). L'Antianalysant en analyse. *Revue Française de Psychanalyse, 36*: 167–184.

Parat, H. (2011). L'Érotique maternelle et l'interdit primaire de l'inceste. *Revue Française de Psychanalyse, 75*: 1609–1614.

Parsons, M. (1996). Recent work by André Green. *International Journal of Psychoanalysis, 77*: 399–340.

Perelberg, R. J. (1995). Feelings and their absence from the analytic setting. *British Journal of Psychotherapy, 12* (2): 212–221.

Perelberg, R. J. (Ed.) (1999). *Psychoanalytic Understanding of Violence and Suicide*. London: Routledge.

Perelberg, R. J. (2003). Full and empty spaces in the analytic process. *International Journal of Psychoanalysis, 84*: 579–592.

Perelberg, R. J. (2004). Narcissistic configurations: Violence and its absence in treatment. *International Journal of Psychoanalysis, 85*: 1065–1079.

Perelberg, R. J. (2005). *Idées directrices pour une psychanalyse contemporaine* by André Green [Book review]. *International Journal of Psychoanalysis, 86*: 207–213.

Perelberg, R. J. (2006). The Controversial Discussions and *après-coup*. *International Journal of Psychoanalysis, 87*: 1199–1220.

Perelberg, R. J. (2008). *Time, Space and Phantasy*. London: Routledge.

Perelberg, R. J. (2009). Murdered father, dead father: Revisiting the Oedipus complex. *International Journal of Psychoanalysis, 90*: 713–732.

Perelberg, R. J. (2013). Paternal function and thirdness in psychoanalysis and legend: Has the future been foretold? *Psychoanalytic Quarterly, 82*: 557–585.

Perelberg, R. J. (2015a). The murder of the dead father as habitus. *Murdered Father, Dead Father: Revisiting the Oedipus Complex* (pp. 163–185). London: Routledge.

Perelberg, R. J. (2015b). On excess, trauma and helplessness: Repetitions and transformations. *International Journal of Psychoanalysis, 96*: 1453–1476.

Pirlot, G., & Cupa, D. (2012). *André Green. Les Grands concepts psychanalytiques*. Paris: Presses Universitaires de France.

Reed, G. S. (2002). The work of the negative. *Journal of the American Psychoanalytic Association, 50*: 343–347.

Reed, G. S., Levine, H. B., & Scarfone, D. (2013). Introduction: From a universe of presences to a universe of absences. In: H. B. Levine, G. S. Reed, & D. Scarfone (Eds.), *Unrepresented States and the Construction of Meaning* (pp. 3–17). London: Karnac.

Stein, R. (1991). *Psychoanalytic Theories of Affect*. New York: Praeger.

Urribarri, F. (2013). *Dialogue avec André Green*. Paris: Editions d'Ithaque.

Viderman, S. (1970). *La Construction de l'espace analytique*. Paris: Denoel.

Winnicott, D. W. (1956). Clinical varieties of transference. In: *Through Paediatrics to Psychoanalysis* (pp. 295–299). London: Hogarth Press, 1975; reprinted London: Karnac, 1984.

Winnicott, D. W. (1960). Ego distortion in terms of true and false self. In: *The Maturational Processes and the Facilitating Environment: Studies in the Theory of Emotional Development* (pp. 140–152). London: Hogarth Press, 1965; reprinted London: Karnac, 1990.

Winnicott, D. W. (1963). Communicating and not communicating leading to a study of certain opposites. In: *The Maturational Processes and the Facilitating Environment: Studies in the Theory of Emotional Development* (pp. 179–192). London: Hogarth Press, 1965; reprinted London: Karnac, 1990.

Winnicott, D. W. (1971a). Creativity and its origins. In: *Playing and Reality* (pp. 65–85). London: Tavistock Publications.

Winnicott, D. W. (1971b). Transitional objects and transitional phenomena. In: *Playing and Reality* (pp. 1–30). London: Tavistock Publications.

Winnicott, D. W. (1971c). The use of an object and relating through identifications. In: *Playing and Reality* (pp. 86–94). London: Tavistock Publications.

Winnicott, D. W. (1974). Fear of breakdown. *International Review of Psycho-Analysis, 1*: 103–107.

CHAPTER ONE

On death and destructiveness

Litza Guttieres-Green

First, I would like to thank you for having organised this conference in memory of my husband, André Green, and for having invited me.

About four years ago, after his last stroke, André gradually stopped working, reading, and listening to music. It then struck me that this man, whose vitality had up until now held fast against the blows to his body, gave up in the struggle against death.

After his death, when my grandchildren asked me where he had gone, I realised that I was unable to answer them, as if I myself did not understand what death was. I told them: "When you die, you are nowhere!" They insisted: "But where is nowhere? In the sky? In Heaven?" Faced with the death of loved ones, we see that "one cannot know what death is, neither consciously nor unconsciously", as André said. For Freud, "death is an abstract concept with a negative content" (Freud, 1923b, p. 58).

Even though we know in theory that we will never again see those we have lost, we cannot conceive of it. We say that they left us, as if it were a voluntary act, and yet they continue to live on in our dreams and memories.

André was also my contemporary, and so I found myself confronted at once with both a painful separation and the prospect of my own end. I had experienced loss when I was young, but the pain of grief gave way, bit by bit, to restlessness and to the pleasures of life. This time, however, I knew I was turning the final page. Growing old means giving up, bit by bit, what makes us live, our commitments regarding love and sublimations. Our projects take on a negative hue: not to deteriorate too much, not to burden our children too much, not to suffer too much. Many of us, frightened more by the loss of our independence and our faculties than by an inconceivable death, and under the illusion of retaining the slipping hold, leave instructions to our children and to our doctor. Surely, as Freud wrote, "the organism wishes to dies only in its own fashion" (Freud, 1920g, p. 39).

We know that Freud did not see death only as an inevitable end to which we must resign ourselves. He thought that it could also be an object of desire, where we escape the sufferings inflicted by life in search of absolute calm.

In *Beyond the Pleasure Principle* (1920g), having witnessed the First World War, Freud introduced, alongside the love and life drives, the death and destruction drives. At first they are turned inward in order to reduce tensions; then these drives mix with the life drives and, diverted towards an external object, they take on the form of destructiveness: "We perceive that for purpose of discharge the instinct of destruction is habitually brought into the service of Eros" (Freud, 1923b, p. 41).

Back then, some psychoanalysts contested his hypothesis, but ever since, we still find ourselves confronted with the same questions that he tried to answer.

Our generation was witness to the horrors of the Second World War, we witnessed the Holocaust, atomic war, we saw the pilots from both sides of the battle lines who shot down planes like toys/ things, forgetting that they were killing kindred men, and then we were shocked by the Nazis' lack of guilt that led Hanna Arendt to conclude the "banality of evil" (Arendt, 1963). And today we find ourselves faced with youth who want to join Jihad, convinced of working towards good through the release of the aggression that inhabits them. We ask ourselves incredulously what pushes human beings, and not necessarily ignorant and barbarian ones, to regress to the point of justifying and committing, with pride and not guilt, acts of destruction that will eventually lead to their own death.

How can they set out, brandishing rifles or strapped with explosives round their hip, in the name of a country, a utopia, or a god, to kill strangers and children whom they consider to be noxious beasts—disobjectalised, to use André's expression.

Freud's texts on destructivity strike us in their lucidity and visionary genius, even as their cold and distant tone perturbs us—when he writes, for example, in "Thoughts for the Times on War and Death": "These impulses in themselves are neither good nor bad" (Freud, 1915b, p. 281); and then, in *Civilization and its Discontents*: ". . . the inborn human inclination to 'badness', to aggressiveness and destructiveness, and so to cruelty as well" (Freud, 1930a, p. 120).

I sometimes watch my grandchildren over the weekend: two brothers, 6 and 9 years old, who are generally affectionate and sweet. But they often argue, cry out in rage, and accuse each other of every wrongdoing: They yell: "He started!" I try to separate them; they regroup quickly and start fighting again. When I scold them, they protest: "But we're playing!" I ask: "Can't you play at anything but war?" and the eldest replies, shrugging his shoulders: "The world anyway has too many people!" I couldn't believe it!

One must come to terms with it: Men are all cut from the same cloth, despite the fact that we want to see evil only in the other. Civilisation has been a long learning process that is continuously called into question. "It is nevertheless surprising that evil should re-emerge with such force in anyone who has been brought up in this way", Freud noted (1915b, p. 281).

While refusing the solution of a god who promises eternal bliss in the ever-after, Freud held that "only religion can answer the question of the purpose of life . . . what men themselves show by their behaviour to be the purpose and intention of their lives. What do they demand of life and wish to achieve in it? . . . They strive after happiness; they want to become happy and to remain so" (Freud, 1930a, p. 76). It unsettles us when Freud places sublimation alongside the death drive, but don't our efforts in war and sacrifice, under the pretence of reforming the world, reveal a reversal of the destruction drive into an erotic component, and vice versa?

Through his clinical work, André came to share the hypothesis of the existence of the death drive, while insisting on the role of the object that unveils the drive, which Freud neglected.

In 1983, André described, alongside life narcissism (which tends towards unity of the self), a death narcissism, which "would be one of the most devastating forms of the death drive" (p. 36). During a seminar in 1994 he raised the "genocide question", which he described as "one of the most extreme forms of discontent in contemporary civilization". He added: "One can no longer consider it as accidental. One is forced to think that we are faced with an endemic, potentially lasting evil that will resurface at every occasion." Indeed, "the destruction of the soul would be the goal of every undertaking of enslavement and domination in the war that opposes it against the other: the stranger, the bad, the hated".

Evil is the antagonist of good. "Why evil?", André asked himself (Green, 1990, pp. 386–387). Every conflict has its scapegoat, responsible for all frustration, and which thus justifies its own extermination. So "once evil is defeated and destroyed, happiness and the sovereign good will reign undisputed" (Green, 1993). To escape remorse, we must be convinced that the death of the enemy will ensure the triumph of good. The problems of violence, of delinquency at ever younger ages, troubled André, as, in case after case, psychoanalysis revealed itself to be of doubtful therapeutic efficacy. He highlighted the frequency of non-neurotic pathologies and the need to struggle on a social level against the organisations that support and favour delinquency or perversions, while recognising that the reach of our efforts is likely to be limited. To quote him: "Current psychoanalytic practice has no problem in identifying unenmeshed forms of destructivity, more or less apparent in serious neurosis and character neurosis, narcissistic structures, borderline cases, etc." (Green, 1986, pp. 52–53).

He pointed out that almost every current clinical study is based on the role of destructivity. Benno Rosenberg, Anne Denis, Rosine Perelberg, Claude Balier, and others have described and discussed the cases of patients guilty of acts of violence.

Recently, the act of the airliner pilot who voluntarily crashed his plane against the mountains, causing the death of 150 people, shocked us. The inquiry concluded premeditated suicide, an act of vengeance against those who hadn't recognised his merits, the ridiculous dream of being spoken about in the papers, a melancholic tragedy, "a pure culture of the death instinct" (Freud, 1920g, p. 53)!

Ensnared by the death drive, the subject aims—not always knowingly—at his own destruction and, by virtue of his ongoing unbinding, that of his ability to think.

André asked himself whether one could conceive of a drive that was un-enmeshed. Eros binds—it even binds destructivity to sadism, it is able to bind in order then to unbind. The death drive is, on the other hand, a radical unbinding after which no possibility of rebinding exists.

Freud reaffirmed in *Civilization and Its Discontents* (1930a) that his hypothesis of the death drive was unavoidable. And André noticed to what extent the *disobjectalising function* is still at work, and how the cultural relativism of today undermines civilisation's possibilities of fighting against the power of destructivity.

In wondering whether the civilising ideal might succeed in saving threatened humanity, André concluded that "civilizing reason can only prevail by recognizing not only the constituent unreason of man, who is its secret shadow, but also man's passionate–instinctual nature, the primary resource of our humanity" (Green, 1993). I shall conclude by returning to the denial of death, that of others as well as our own. To accept it, men need hope of surviving, some in an imaginary hereafter, others in the memory of those who will come after them. To bear the effects of our aggression, we must justify it through idealised aims so that—enmeshed—it does not destroy us. It seems to me that psychoanalytic work aims at this enmeshment of destructivity with Eros.

Thank you for having given me the opportunity to reflect upon the causes and the effects of the persistence of this "discontent in civilization".

References

Arendt, H. (1963). *Eichmann in Jerusalem.* New York: Viking Press.

Freud, S. (1915b). Thoughts for the times on war and death. *Standard Edition, 14:* 275–300.

Freud, S. (1920g). *Beyond the Pleasure Principle. Standard Edition, 18:* 7–64.

Freud, S. (1923b). *The Ego and the Id. Standard Edition, 19:* 12–66.

Freud, S. (1930a). *Civilization and Its Discontents. Standard Edition*, 21: 57–146.

Green, A. (1983). *Narcissisme de vie. Narcissisme de mort*. Paris: Éditions de Minuit.

Green, A. (1986). *La Pulsion de mort*. Paris: Presses Universitaires de France.

Green, A. (1990). Pourquoi le mal. In: *La Folie privée. Psychanalyse des cas-limites*. Paris: Gallimard.

Green, A. (1993). Culture(s) et civilisation(s), malaise ou maladie? *Revue Française de Psychanalyse*, 4: 1029–1056.

CHAPTER TWO

Negative hallucinations, dreams, and hallucinations: the framing structure and its representation in the analytic setting

Rosine Jozef Perelberg

The framing structure

Green states that when holding her infant, the mother leaves the impression of her arms on the child, and this constitutes a framing structure that, in her absence, contains the loss of the perception of the maternal object and a negative hallucination of it. The framing structure is the outcome of the internalisation of the maternal environment created by maternal care. It is the "primordial matrix of the cathexis to come" (Green, 1986b, p. 166). The capacity for the negative hallucination of the mother lies at the origins of representation; it is against the background of negativity that future representations of the object are inscribed. This is the role of the negative in its structuring function (Green, 2005a, p. 161;[1] 2005b). From this perspective, negative hallucination precedes all theory of representation. The negative hallucination creates a potential space for the representation and investment of new objects and the conditions in which the activities of thinking and symbolisation can take place.[2] In marking the role of the absent other in the constitution of the psyche, Green is following the traditions of both Winnicott and Bion. This is an absence as "an intermediary situation between presence . . . and loss" (Urribarri, 2005, p. 205). This leads to Green's statement that "the Psyche is the relationship between two bodies in which one is absent" (1995, pp. 69–76).[3]

The negative hallucination of the mother is a precondition for Freud's hallucinatory wish-fulfilment, for images, for phantasy life, and for thinking. It is also an indication of thirdness, as the mother's absence implicitly poses the question: "Where does she go, when she goes away?" This is an implicit reference to the father. It is to him, as her lover, that she goes. The mother's absence and the activity of phantasy that her absence gives rise to within the framing structure lies at the heart of Green's formulation about the psychoanalytic setting itself.

What happens if these processes fail to take place and if a traumatic intrusion does not allow for absence that would enable a psychic space to be solidly constituted? What are the consequences for the beginnings of phantasy life if the mother is too terrifying for the child, like the psychotic mother, so that the child cannot internalise its framing structure? In his formulation of the "dead mother complex", Green (1986b) outlines the way in which maternal traumatism, the mother's depression and withdrawal from the child, has consequences for the constitution of the child's psyche, leaving psychic holes in the unconscious, a loss of meaning—no-thing, in Bion's terms (Bion, 1965, p. 79)—and an impairment of the capacity to represent and to separate the intrapsychic from the intersubjective. There are implications for a theory of technique in that the role of the analyst is not that of interpreting what is already there in the mind of the patient; the analytic task becomes a process of constructing such meaning (Perelberg, 2003, 2015b). Any manifestation of hatred in such an analysis is a consequence of this massive decathexis and secondary to it; if the analyst's interpretations are centred on the attacks on the setting, they will be futile and will not address the main problem (Green, 1986a).

Too much absence, Green suggests, leads to the sentiment of solitude, helplessness, and despair; a separation that lasts too long leads to the decathexis of the object (Winnicott, 1971), as the patient's mind becomes filled with death, absence, or amnesia. An over-presence that is too frightening leads to a disorganising, incomprehensible, claustrophobic internal and external world.

The following clinical vignette is an example of an analysis where one gained access to a terrifying maternal imago in the vicissitudes of the transference and countertransference.

Clinical vignette: Carolina

Carolina's analysis: Tearing the fabric of the dream

One Wednesday morning Carolina came to her session and said:

Carolina: "I can remember a dream that was horrendous. One of those dreams I tend to have and never remember.

Two words stand out: 'against abortion'. In the dream *I was struggling to tear the fabric of the dream. It all felt reasonable in the dream. The words kept being repeated in my head throughout, as if it was chanting a (refrain). A knife was going to be pinned through my back. I was half asleep throughout and was telling myself that it was just a dream. I was diving. There was also this cheese that had melted, and words were appearing written in cheese. Then I was diving in green murky waters. All the time my dream was like a piece of fabric, and I was trying to tear a way out of it. The waters were mud. I was mud. In the mud there were fish, seahorses, crabs—all these things in the mud that turned into glass, shards of glass. They were cutting me inside.*

It was a horrific dream. My half-awake state lasted for a long time until I could sleep again."

[She half laughed.]

[Very long silence.]

I commented that it was horrific, and yet she was half laughing: I wonder if the laughter became a way of disowning such a horrific dream.

She said that it was just a dream.

Analyst: "It is an experience that you went through for a long time during the night."

[Silence.]

Carolina: "I can't think seriously about it. . . But it was scary to be in my room as I went through it . . ."

[I was thinking about her coming in with her usual smiling face, in a rush . . .]

Analyst: "Perhaps there is a link between these dreams that don't feel real and your constant state of activity, trying to escape from this horrific dream life."

Carolina said that it reminded her of a dream that she had had a long time ago.

"I was in a horror film, a pastiche of Scream. It was in a big house with a big garden, a perfect setting for a horror dream. Eventually the ambulance arrived. Someone had gone missing, and it was me. There was a crazy lunatic murderer out there. The ambulance finally came, they were carrying someone on a stretcher who had died, and it was me. There was a balloon-shaped membrane coming out of me, obscuring my face. I think that membrane was full of blood that was threatening to burst out. It was just like when I was trying to tear out of the dream."

[Silence.]

Analyst: "It is so horrific; in several ways you have to keep out of the dream. It is a film, and you are watching what is happening." [I was addressing her relationship to the dream rather than the content.]

Carolina: "I am frightened but I am also frightening. Like in today's dream the mud is me. It is an engulfing thing that prevents me from moving. It is more comfortable for me to think of myself as the scared creature. The 'it' that scares me is the unknown factor of how mad I am. I associate this dream to a Lorca play that was made into a film: *Blood Wedding*. The mother in this film anticipated all the horror that was about to happen. She said: 'There is a scream in my ear that is always rising up.'

She anticipated all the blood that was to follow, and she could not do anything about it. The mother's scream is of anguish and foreboding: she anticipates it all and cannot stop it. My fear is that if I get in touch with it all, I will never get out of it, I will never be able to stop the anguish, the tears, and the overwhelming sadness." [She cries.]

She does not really scream, Carolina adds.

Analyst: "The horrific world that you connect with a mother's screams that intrudes into you, your heart; you fear you cannot do anything about it."

[Silence.]

Carolina: "I wonder why this dream happens now."

Analyst: "When thinking about the knife in your back, I wonder if it is fear of me too, and of what is on my mind" [thinking of the very first consultation, when she had talked about *Fawlty Towers*, in which a seemingly inoffensive Portuguese waiter was apparently capable of murder].

Carolina: "I wonder about the word 'abortion' in the dream. I know that my mother wanted to abort me . . ."

[Silence.]

Analyst [I had in mind the fact that I had cancelled two sessions this week]: "I am thinking of this week, with just three sessions that feel so disturbing. Like an abortion."

In this session, there is a profound link between the nightmare of the previous night, a repetitive childhood dream, and the experience in the transference of a maternal imago that evokes death rather than life.

Background

Carolina was the youngest of four children, the other three being boys. The family was originally from a Latin American country. Carolina had moved to London a few years earlier because of her work, and the analysis took place in her maternal language. Carolina remembers feeling frightened and confused in the world as a child, not fully understanding what was going on around her and the nature of people's relationships to each other. From very early on she remembers feeling terrified of her mother, whose behaviour felt unpredictable. She herself felt monstrous and thought her mother hated her. She remembers being kept up till late at night watching horror movies with her mother, who would then pretend that she was herself a monster—Dracula, or a vampire—and then laugh in a most violent way. Carolina was not sure whether she was more frightened of the monster or of not knowing whether her mother was being serious or joking. Carolina felt that she would have preferred her mother to actually be a monster to the uncertainty of not knowing. She felt unable to separate reality from the nightmarish world of the horror films.

Carolina was told by her mother that she had wanted to abort her; her mother also found her a difficult baby, who was always crying and dissatisfied. Her mother taught her not to cry by closing the bedroom door and leaving her to cry until she stopped.

Between the ages of 6 and 9, her mother developed an extensive narrative about witches. The world was populated by witches, good and bad. She was a good witch; the bad witches were always trying to snatch children, so one had to be careful. At night her mother went out on her broomstick. Sometimes Carolina went to the window to try to catch sight of her, and several times she thought she had seen her flying by.

When the family moved to another city, Carolina's mother told her that their new home had been built in a cemetery. There was a graveyard opposite the house, and she thought that it was an evil street. Carolina was terrified at night as she lay awake, listening to deep clanking noises coming from the nearby market. Her mother said that they were killing animals; sometimes Carolina thought that they were killing humans. The world felt terrifying and unpredictable.

Carolina did not have much contact with her two older brothers, quite a few years her senior, who had remained in their city of origin. Her younger brother, in contrast to herself, seemed to be a happy being. He was liked by everyone, and he ran around, carefree and contented. As she grew up, her father provided a sense of a minimal protection when he was at home. He worked long hours and used to come home very late. Carolina experienced him, nevertheless, as distant and demanding and felt that she was a disappointment to him. Once she remembers going to his office on the top floor, where she was expected to do an old paper as practise for a school entrance exam. The problem was that it was about fractions, which she hadn't yet studied and didn't know anything about. So when her father told her to pick an answer from the multiple-choice test, she assumed that the big numbers would be the right answers. Her father was frustrated with her, saying: "No, no, no, pick another one." She had no idea what she was supposed to do. This interaction seemed to characterise some of her experience of being in the world, and later on in the analysis she consistently felt she was being asked to solve fractions, which she didn't understand. She tried to overcome this experience by frantically pretending to fit in.

Carolina was nevertheless very bright and worked hard at school. She did well and was accepted by a prestigious university in her country; when she finished, she embarked on a successful career of her choice. At the time she came for analysis, Carolina had come to London to work for a prestigious law firm.

The analysis

On the eve of starting her five-times-a-week analysis, Carolina phoned me to say that her father had died. Her boss at work had given her a month off, so that she could travel abroad to be with her mother. The beginning of her analysis was thus marked by her father's death and by her absence in order to be with her mother. In many ways this configuration set the tone of the early months of her analysis, marked by the register of the repetition compulsion. The father had gone, and we were both going to be left to deal with her being with the mad mother.

During the first few months of our work together, Carolina was in a traumatised state in response to her father's death. Progressively I realised that there was a strong sense of absence, of lack of contact, of bewilderment as she spoke about feeling lost in the world. At the time she used to have terrifying nightmares, of which she would have few recollections apart from waking up screaming in terror in the middle of the night. These nightmares without words allude to the negative hallucination of thought and to Carolina's inability to express herself in words that conveyed meaning. They belonged to the order of that which was, until then, unrepresented. In the sessions I was struck by her constant activity at work: she was always in "action mode". Her narrative in the sessions had an evacuatory quality. She could speak continuously for the 50 minutes of each session without giving me any space to make a comment. There was a force in her speech that some time later I referred to as a machine gun (as it evoked a sense of murder and war). In the countertransference I sometimes felt totally squashed, empty, and depleted at the end of such sessions.

What Carolina brought to her analysis was the experience of not possessing a thinking structure that allowed her to process experiences into thoughts. Once she had a dream in which *she had lost the top of her skull, and there were worms inside her head, spilling out.* Coming to analysis and exposing herself to the mind of another as well as her own was the most dangerous situation she could put herself in.

The nightmare I described at the beginning captures so many aspects of her experience of being at work and in analysis. Trying to tear the fabric of the dream represents her attempt to get rid of this experience of being trapped inside the mother's body, the mother's mind, her own mind and that of the analyst. Her mother had wanted to abort her: she is experienced as the source of death, terrors, and nightmares, rather than as life-giving. The waters of her womb are murky and contain fish, seahorses, crabs: primitive things, not a human foetus. They turn into glass—shards of glass that cut from the inside. The world of *Blood Wedding* is tragic: the men die in knife fights, and the women survive on their own. They are left with the mother's scream. The characters do not have names but are referred to in terms of their positions in the family: Mother, Father, Brother, Bride and Bridegroom. This is the world of Spanish South America, with the inherent violence of the Spanish conquest and later consecutive dictatorships. It is this tragic, excessive, nameless world that we attempt to navigate in the analysis (Perelberg, 2015b).[4]

In the present, too, Carolina was always left confused after her interactions with her mother as to whether something had or had not really happened. This was minimally present in the transference as well as in the countertransference, although a few years were to go by before it became possible to experience this more directly. An association that occurred to me in that initial phase of our work together was derived from the film *Gaslight*, in which the victim is gradually manipulated into doubting her own reality.[5] *Time Out* wrote about the 1940 version of the film: "Lurking menace hangs in the air like a fog, the atmosphere is electric, and Wynyard suffers exquisitely as she struggles to keep dementia at bay" (in Wikipedia).

The hallucination of the knife

Three years into her analysis, Carolina had a hallucination of a knife that persecuted her throughout a whole weekend. She said that it was neither a dream nor a vision: this knife floated around her all the time. She could not get rid of it, and she continued to see it in her dreams as well as when she woke up. She felt terrified, claustrophobic, and very disturbed. In my countertransference I also felt alarmed and anxious that the psychotic part of her personality was becoming more prominent.

The meaning of the knife was overdetermined. Carolina had met a man and had been invited to spend the weekend at his mother's house. The knife was an attack on everything that was nascent at the time: This knife enabled her to cut herself off into a narcissistic enclosure where everything else paled into insignificance and became meaningless. It felt like a fundamental "no" she was saying to herself and to me, a pure culture of the work of the negative: "I can say no to everything."

The knife, ever present throughout the weekend, reminded me of *Blood Wedding*. The Mother says, at the beginning of Act I: "The knife, the knife . . . Damn all of them and the scoundrel who invented them . . . even the tiniest knife . . . and mattocks and pitchforks . . . Everything that can cut a man's body . . ." (Lorca, 1987, p. 3). There was something inexorably present and foreboding about it. One was left in a universe provided by the crazy Mother. Could analysis introduce a difference to the mother's predictions?

This episode also reminded me of the Wolf Man's negative hallucination of cutting his finger off.[6]

The hallucination of the knife took place over a weekend, away from the analysis. It was to be expected that we would eventually confront something in the consulting room itself.

The human-sized wasp

In a session a few weeks later, a wasp got into the room and was buzzing around the window, sometimes circling the room. I could sense Carolina's paralysis and terror but did not say anything. I thought that we were both being enveloped by a kind of claustrophobic, paralyzing terror that could not be put into words.

The atmosphere was extremely tense, and I waited in a silence that persisted until the end of the session. "Lurking menace hangs in the air like a fog, the atmosphere is electric . . ."

At the following session Carolina told me that she had seen a woman-sized wasp hanging by the door throughout the session and had felt paralysed.

> *Carolina:* "The giant human-sized wasp was definitely by the door. There was a poised elegance about it as it was hanging there. I was thinking that I am carrying on talking here, you try to introduce another point of view, and I feel like I'm being attacked. You say it very gently, politely, and all I can hear is the attack. It is very real.
>
> If there is a frequent image I associate with my mother, it is that of a Rottweiler on a chain, barking and barking and the sharp teeth showing, trying to get rid of the chain in order to attack you and kill you. My mother would show me her Dracula teeth when I was older to scare me, but she told me that she did it even when I was a baby, and I would cry . . . like the human-sized wasp I saw here. It was not like the Rottweiler straining at its lead. It is straining because it wants to kill you. The wasp is more meditative, biding its time. But it is also dangerous. It can eventually kill you."

> *Analyst:* "What there is in common is the sense of danger and threat."

> *Carolina:* "The wasp had not yet decided if it was going to kill you. It is not as violently terrifying. When there was a wasp in the room, I couldn't relax, as I couldn't predict what would happen . . . Some sessions I can leave unscathed, but I never know. Outside I can keep an eye on them, but they are more elusive and harder to pin down. Here is the same, meaning that it is harder to pin down for me, it buzzes away. I think of them as dangerous."

> *Analyst:* "This is your experience of being here: fear, danger . . . Of me, but perhaps also of yourself."

> *Carolina:* "The worst is to think of all this aggression in me . . ."

Images, dreams, hallucinations: some reflections

In *The Interpretation of Dreams*, Freud postulated "conditions of representability" "as one of the characteristics of the dream work" (1900a, p. 499). Thoughts are expressed in images that condense a multitude of thoughts or people, giving rise to "composite images" (p. 324). Images are the oldest form of registering an experience; they are closer to the unconscious. The word "image" is derived from "imago", the representation of the ancestor at the very moment of its disappearance—that is, at the moment of mourning (Rolland, 2015, p. 107). The presence of an image is linked to the absence of the object. This absence is at the origin of the hallucinatory wish-fulfilment of infancy whereby the baby tries to reproduce the experience of satisfaction.

> An essential component of this experience of satisfaction is a particular perception (that of nourishment, in our example), the mnemic image of which remains associated thenceforward with the memory trace of the excitation produced by the need. As a result of the link that has thus been established, next time this need arises a psychical impulse will at once emerge which will seek to re-cathect the mnemic image of the perception and to re-evoke the perception itself, that is to say, to re-establish the situation of the original satisfaction. [Freud, 1900a, pp. 565–566]

In "Negation", Freud postulates that images originated from perceptual experiences:

> . . . all presentations originate from perceptions and are repetitions of them. Thus originally the mere existence of a presentation was a guarantee of the reality of what was presented. The antithesis between subjective and objective does not exist from the first. It only comes into being from the fact that thinking possesses the capacity to bring before the mind once more something that has once been perceived, by reproducing it as a presentation without the external object having still to be there. [Freud, 1925h, p. 237]

Images are polysemic and irradiate in multiple directions, evoking different layers of experience. The analytic process brings forth, from time to time, images that are like the mythogram of the individual history in that they organise the affective experience of the individual (Rolland, 2015, p. 143).

In ordinary development one can trace a sequence from the experience of satisfaction, the absence of the object, the negative hallucination in its structuring function, to hallucinatory wish-fulfilment—all of which lie at the origin of representation.

Images are the material of the hallucination wish-fulfilment, of dreams, phantasies, and works of art, but they can also be the stuff of hallucinations, as in the case of Freud's hysterics, the most famous of whom might be Anna O., who was treated by Breuer (Freud, 1895d [1893–95]). She had hallucinations of snakes when she was looking after her father, who was ill and was about to die, leaving her at the mercy of a melancholic maternal imago (Perelberg, 1999a). These hallucinations represent a failure in the capacity for an internal, unconscious representation that are turned into perceptions. Freud considered that the aim of the treatment was to replace such images with narratives that would tell their stories.

Hallucinations can be understood as a first attempt at self-cure, as in the Schreber case (Freud, 1911c [1910]). The delusional formation "is in reality an attempt at recovery, a process of reconstruction" (p. 71). "This attempt at recovery, which observers mistake for the disease itself, does not, as in paranoia, make use of projection, but employs a hallucinatory (hysterical) mechanism" (p. 77).[7]

Bion understood hallucinations as the outcome of mental processes that destroyed alpha-elements and reduced them to fragments that cannot be thought about but have to be evacuated. They are projected into the outside world, giving rise to bizarre objects. However, the component of self-cure is also present in Bion's formulations. He believes that what is evacuated in hallucinations are sensory elements that still have some elements of meaning attached to them: "The 'peculiarity' of the dream to the psychotic is not its irrationality, incoherence, and fragmentation, but its revelation of objects which are felt by the patient to be whole objects and therefore fit and proper reason for the powerful feelings of guilt and depression" (Bion, 1958, p. 80). Thus for him, too, images have a curative dimension.

My patient's hallucination of the knife indicated an aspect of her experience that had remained foreclosed in her life, a terror of a primitive, murderous maternal imago and her own identification with this mother.[8] The production of a hallucination, however, meant that something was also active in the present, in the immediacy of the transference. In the manner of dreams, there are at least two different sources at work: a mnemic trace inscribed in infancy linked to a traumatism and a current perception that has a capacity to be linked to the mnemic trace. It is therefore multiple representations that give rise to an image (see Birksted-Breen, 2012). In the subsequent hallucination of the wasp, the fear of unpredictability in myself and in her is projected onto the wasp that was buzzing in an arbitrary way around the room. Through her hallucination my patient deposited that wasp in the corner of the room, by the door, where she could keep an eye on it. The possibility of danger was dramatised, but it was now under her omnipotent control. A significant transformation took place between the hallucination of the knife, which indicated a moment when she felt herself to be in mortal danger, and the hallucination of the wasp, a few weeks later, where the danger was experienced as more under her control.

If negative hallucination is the common matrix between dreams and hallucinations, they cannot be superimposed on each other (Green, 1999, p. 276). It is my belief that, in contrast to a dream image, which is a product of condensation and displacement and an outcome of the dream work, when one is dealing with hallucinations, meaning has yet to be achieved. Freud believed that while images condense, hallucinations decompose through splitting (1911c [1910], p. 48). Dream images are internal, the products of psychic reality; hallucinations are an expression of unprocessed material that has been expelled and is experienced as coming from external reality. Schreber's fear of the end of the world was the projection of an internal catastrophe (p. 70); his "rays of god" are a projection of his libidinal cathexes (p. 78). What is unpleasure and alien is located as external to the ego: "what was abolished internally returns from without" (p. 71). In his paper on negation there is an emphasis on the mechanism of expulsion.

Bion (1958) has drawn a distinction between psychotic and hysterical hallucinations. This difference is directly related to an increase in the patient's capacity to tolerate depression. The psychotic hallucination contains elements analogous to part-objects; the hysterical hallucination contains whole objects and is associated with depression.

I would suggest that another differentiation may be that whereas the conflict for the psychotic is between life and death, in the hysterical hallucination it is between love and hate. Both, I believe, contain aspects of remembering. Might it be that Carolina moved between the two? Whereas the hallucination of the knife belonged more to the psychotic part of her personality, with the lurking possibility of murder, might the human-sized wasp belong more to the hysterical register? The wasp was clearly an association to an object, to her mother, to me, and to herself. Some analytic work took place during the time between the two that had transformed the images into words, from the lethal possibility of murder to the experience of more potentially controlled danger.

De Masi, Davalli, Giustino, and Pergami (2015) have indicated that in hallucinations there is a withdrawal from external reality into a sensorial mode. One is dealing with pure sensoriality that has not reached representation or symbolisation (Segal, 1957). According to these authors, "during the hallucinatory experience, the patient does not think, he *sees* or *feels*" (De Masi et al., 2015, p. 313, italics in the original). They also quote from Perceval, for whom the hallucinatory state requires a position of passive acquiescence (p. 308). I can relate this idea to an aspect of Carolina's experience of compliance throughout her life.

Green has suggested that in the treatment of non-neurotic patients, one is dealing not with an economy of unconscious desire, but with a "logic of despair" (Urribarri, 2013, p. 21). This logic is less organised than that of the primary process and has to contend with unprocessed elements coming from the id. Thinking is dominated by the work of the negative (Green, 1999). The aim of the analytic work is to transform hallucinations into words that create a narrative about the patient's history, transforming delirium into play and death into absence.

In the case of such patients, it is a failure of hallucinatory wish-fulfilment that is the basic model for an understanding of the psyche. This failure is the outcome of a traumatic encounter with the primary object. It is not possible to invest the mnemic trace, because of the pain or terror that it will provoke. Rather than evoking an experience of pleasure, it is an experience of distress that comes to the fore. Psychic reality is decathected; the patient withdraws into a "personal, bodily and sensory space of his own" (Urribarri, 2013, p. 293). Mental functioning becomes restricted, cutting off more mature functions. Words are treated as things, as Freud suggested in his paper on the unconscious. The patient is not present in her own discourse and in the session; she also feels like a prisoner. Passivation, the process whereby the patient submits herself to the analytic care, is almost impossible (Green, 1986a).

Paul Williams has written about patients who have suffered an experience of "incorporation of an invasive object", a primitive introjection of aspects of an object that creates an experience of inundation that can give rise to personality disturbance (Williams, 2004).[9] He refers to this process as a form of "proto-identification" that takes place in early infancy and expresses a failure of containment and maternal alpha-function (Bion, 1962). The infant incorporates these violent projections as part of his own mental representational system, and normal identification processes are disrupted. An impairment of the development of the sense of self takes place. The outcome of the early trauma undergone by such patients is expressed in "an amalgam of inchoate experiences, the residuum or precipitate of which may correspond to the 'foreign body' experience lodged in the unconscious and in the body and which lacks mental representational status" (Williams, 2004, p. 1342). Here I have suggested that the production of the images that take on a hallucinatory form become an achievement of the analysis, at the origin of representation of such experiences.

There is an intrinsic link between the framing structure as the place for symbolisation and the analytic experience that will reproduce aspects of the patient's experience with the primary object. The framing structure is not perceptible as such, but only through the productions that it gives rise to in the setting (Green, 1999). It is in the *après-coup* of an analysis that one has access to the traces left by the traumatic, archaic past, some of which will find representation for the first time in the here and now of the analytic process (Perelberg, 2006, 2007, 2011, 2015b).

This leads me to underline an aspect of any analytic treatment, which is its dramatic dimension. Since Breuer and Freud's statement that hysterics suffer mainly from reminiscences (Freud, 1895d [1893–95]) and Freud's work "Remembering, Repeating and Working Through" (1914g), the idea that psychic conflicts can be expressed in ways other than words has become familiar in psychoanalysis. At this point in their work, however, Freud and Breuer saw the symptom as a repetition of the past. Later, Freud was to understand the phenomenon of transference more fully in terms of the links between the there-and-then and the here-and-now. Transference is overdetermined—like Proust's madeleine, which emerges out of a phenomenon of metaphoric and metonymic irradiation, associating several moments, places, and memories and ultimately expressing the infantile desire of the narrator himself (Kristeva, 1996; Perelberg, 2008).

It is my belief that the analytic situation has a dramatic dimension and is by definition traumatic because it evokes the state of helplessness of the new-born infant (*Hilflosigkeit*), which is the prototype of the traumatic situation and at the origin of the experience of anxiety (Perelberg, 2007). It is in this context that the relationship with the primordial object is brought forth.

Transference is filled with our patients' desires, which are linked to their unconscious phantasies and infantile sexuality, ruled now by the compulsion to repeat.

In his *Introductory Lectures on Psycho-Analysis*, Freud had already stated that, in traumatic neurosis,

> patients regularly repeat the traumatic situation in their dreams; where hysteriform attacks occur that admit of an analysis, we find that the attack corresponds to a complete transplanting of the patient into the traumatic situation. It is as though these patients had not finished with the traumatic situation, as though they were still faced by it as an immediate task which has not been dealt with. [Freud, 1916–17, p. 274]

In *Beyond the Pleasure Principle*, when briefly discussing traumatic dreams, Freud postulates:

> Now dreams occurring in traumatic neuroses have the characteristic of repeatedly bringing the patient back into the situation of his accident, a situation from which he wakes up in another fright. [Freud, 1920g, p. 13]

Under the register of the compulsion to repeat, the original traumatic situation is being lived again in dreams in the present (see also Perelberg, 2000). Later (1933a) Freud will say that these traumatic dreams generate anxiety.

In 1920 there was, therefore, an important substitution in Freud's model, an emphasis on representations being replaced by one on the act (Green, 2002, p. 163). These ideas are specifically relevant to a modern conceptualisation of the analytic situation and the understanding that patients act rather than remember.

The repetition of traumatic situations is a characteristic not only of traumatic dreams, but of any dreams, and of the analytic situation itself. One is no longer referring to a setting wherein the patient speaks and the analyst interprets, but to a dramatic encounter wherein patient and analyst will minimally repeat an interaction that is relevant to the patient's past.[10] The challenge for any analysis is to introduce a transformation in the narrative anticipated by the compulsion to repeat.[11]

Further developments

Five years into the analysis Carolina met a man, married him, and became pregnant. In the initial months of her pregnancy her sense of persecution increased. Things changed when she was able to see the first scan. The baby became a living human being for her, and at this point her dreams took on a more human quality. Carolina became progressively more excited about the pregnancy.

> *Carolina:* "The changes in my body feel mysterious and magical. I never imagined I'd feel all right in this way. I am hoping that all these changes that are happening are so that I can breast-feed. I am sure that I can feel this way because I am coming here."
>
> *Analyst:* "Perhaps you came to analysis in order to be able to have a baby."

The dream from the beginning of her analysis came to my mind: the mother who announces death; also, the words "against abortion". Carolina could perhaps now see herself as a mother who wanted to be life-giving and not an announcer of death.

Notes

1. "I make the assumption that the child (whatever culture he is born in) is held by the mother against her body. When contact with the mother's body is broken, what remains of this experience is the trace of bodily contact—as a rule the mother's arms—which constitutes a framing structure sheltering the loss of the perception of the maternal object, *in the form of a negative hallucination of it*" (Green, 2005a, p. 161, italics in the original).

2. "Are we not justified in inferring that the negative hallucination of the mother, without in any way representing anything, has made the conditions for representation possible" (Green, 2001, p. 86)?

3. It is crucial to distinguish the negative hallucination of the mother as the requirement for normal processes of development from what may be understood as a negative hallucination of thought that refers to states of emptiness and holes in the psyche, as in borderline structures (see also Pirlot & Cupa, 2012, pp. 57–59). The negative hallucination of the mother, at the beginnings of psychic life, is to be distinguished from the negative hallucination of the object in terms of the denial of its existence, an expression of foreclosure. One is distinguishing the role of the negative in its structuring function from its destructive aspects (see Perelberg, 2015a). Freud stated in 1917: "I may add . . . that any attempt to explain hallucination would have to start out from the negative rather than positive hallucination" (1917d [1915], p. 232). An example of a negative hallucination of the object may be found in Perelberg, 2003. I gave the example of my patient Simon, who revealed that he had, on occasions, parked his car in front of my house to watch me and my family, although he had consistently fallen asleep before he saw any of us. I understood this as expressing "his conflict between the wish to be seen and not to be seen, between wanting to know and not to know, a reminder of the Wolf Man's wish to know nothing, to foreclose. When Simon had parked his car in front of my house, the aim was to observe in order to eliminate the object, the third (negative hallucination), in this case, knowledge of the existence of my family and my life independent from him." (Perelberg, 2003, pp. 580–581).

4. At the The Greening of Psychoanalysis Conference, Howard Levine suggested that "the unrepresented never appears in pure form, but, rather, 'soldered to' or 'wrapped around' the represented and it does cause absences, and disorganizes one's psyche and capacity to think. This produces symptoms, which are dealt with by secondary symptom formation. Patients might then develop secondary symptoms (that are organized and represented) following the thinking deficits and structural deficits that are the heirs to effacement (unrepresented), decathexis and negative hallucination" (personal communication, 2015).

5. Film precis: Alice Barlow is murdered by an unknown man, who then ransacks her house, looking for her famous valuable rubies. The house remains empty for years, until newlyweds Paul and Bella Mallen move in. Bella soon finds herself misplacing small objects, and before long Paul has her believing that she is losing her sanity. B. G. Rough, a former detective involved in the original murder investigation, immediately suspects him of Alice Barlow's murder. Paul uses the gas lamps to search the closed-off upper floors, which causes the lamps in the rest of the house to dim slightly. When Bella comments on this, he tells her she is imagining things. Bella is persuaded she is hearing noises, unaware that Paul enters the upper floors from the house next-door. This is part of a larger pattern of deception to which Bella is subjected. It is revealed that Paul is the wanted Louis Bauer, who has returned to the house to search for the rubies he was unable to find after the murder [https:// en.wikipedia.org/wiki/Gaslight_(1940_film)]. "Gaslighting" describes a form of psychological abuse in which the victim is gradually manipulated into doubting his or her own sanity. The term originates from the 1938 stage play *Gaslight*, by Patrick Hamilton, and its two film adaptations.

6. "I was playing in the garden near my nurse and was carving with my pocket-knife in the bark of one of the walnut-trees that come into my dream as well. Suddenly, to my unspeakable terror, I noticed that I had cut through the little finger of my (right or left?) hand, so that it was only hanging on by its skin. I felt no pain, but great fear. I did not venture to say anything to my nurse, who was only a few paces distant, but I sank down on the nearest seat and sat there incapable of casting another glance at my finger. At last I calmed down, took a look at the finger, and saw that it was entirely uninjured" (Freud, 1914a, p. 205).

7. In this text Freud attempts to distinguish between "dementia praecox", which produces violent hallucinations, and paranoia, which employs projection. He suggests that dementia praecox indicates a point of fixation between auto-erotism and object love, whereas paranoia indicates a regression to the state of narcissism. Freud concludes, however, that paranoid and schizophrenic phenomena may be combined in different proportions. In the Schreber case, he suggests, one can identify the production of hallucinations and distinguish it from the paranoid mechanisms of projection (Freud, 1911c [1910], pp. 77–78).

8. Some other clinical examples that illustrate the terror of this archaic mother may be found in Perelberg (1995, 1998, 1999b, 2003, 2015b).See also Kohon (2010).

9. In *Studies on Hysteria* (1895d [1893–95]), Freud refers to the traumatic thus: "We presume . . . that the psychical trauma—or more precisely the memory of the trauma—acts like a foreign body which long after its entry must continue to be regarded as an agent that is still at work" (p. 6). Freud is pointing out the way in which what is traumatic is unabsorbable by representation and inaccessible to symbolisation.

10. This is the paradigmatic shift introduced by Freud with his *Beyond the Pleasure Principle* (1920g) and "Constructions in Analysis" (1937d). In the British Psychoanalytical Society, key papers that have continued to explore these fundamental issues include those by Heimann (1950), Sandler (1976), Segal (1977), King (1978), and Joseph (1985). Sandler has delineated the various stages of development of the concept of projective identification. With Klein, it refers to a process that takes place in phantasy. A second stage may be identified with the developments described in the work of Heimann (1950), Racker (1968), and Grinberg (1962), whereby the countertransference reaction on the part of the analyst becomes a possible source of information about what is occurring in the mind of the patient. In the work of Bion, this extension of the understanding of the concept finds expression in his concepts of the container and reverie: what is projected onto the analyst is contained and transformed by the work of reverie on the part of the analyst. A fourth stage may be found in the work of Sandler himself (1976) and of Joseph (1985), both of whom indicate how what is projected onto the analyst provokes a response in the analyst, who is "nudged" to respond in a certain way (see also Spillius, 1992). In what concerns dreams, Kohon (2000) has suggested that these may be a form of acting out. Perelberg has suggested that "dreams contain a condensed narrative about the transference relationship and encapsulate a narrative that will unfold as the analysis progresses" (2000, p. 109).

11. When I presented this chapter to the Scientific Meeting at the British Psychoanalytical Society on 15 March 2017, Josh Cohen noted my use of the analytic silence in the session and suggested that this silence gave expression to the theory of the hallucinated frame – it was the introduction of an "interval", both temporal and spatial, which brought a measure of differentiation to the patient's chaotic, and undifferentiated, dream life. He suggested the following: "There is an analogue to the negative holding structure in various modern art experiments, an example of which is Kasimir Malevich's *Black Square*, which is about the relation of figure to ground. The black square requires a minimal background to emerge – a kind of holding structure, without which there is no perception of a differentiated figure, so no black square. Another example would be Robert Rauschenberg's *Erased de Kooning* – Willem de Kooning gave him a pencil drawing, which he meticulously erased, and the marks left were the artwork. Our attention is taken away from the representation to the conditions that make it possible (the paper/'holding structure')." Thus, the silence of the analyst itself might have been a form of structuring interval that enabled a differentiated self to emerge. Cohen links these ideas to Lewin's 1948 paper on the dream screen as the imperceptible background onto which dreams are projected (Cohen, 2013, pp. 186–187). Sara Flanders (personal communication, 2017) made a similar link between my use of silence in the sessions and Lewin's text.

References

Bion, W. R. (1958). On hallucination. In: *Second Thoughts* (pp. 65–85). London: Heinemann, 1967; reprinted London: Karnac, 1984.

Bion, W. R. (1962). A theory of thinking. In: *Second Thoughts* (pp. 110–119). London: Heinemann, 1967; reprinted London: Karnac, 1984. [First published as: The psycho-analytic study of thinking. *International Journal of Psychoanalysis, 43*: 306–310.]

Bion, W. R. (1965). *Transformations*. London: Heinemann; reprinted London: Karnac, 1984.

Birksted-Breen, D. (2012). Taking time: The tempo of psychoanalysis. *International Journal of Psychoanalysis, 93*: 819–835.

Cohen, J. (2013). *The Private Life: Why We Remain in the Dark*. London: Granta Books.

De Masi, F., Davalli, C., Giustino, G., & Pergami, A. (2015). Hallucinations in the psychotic state: Psychoanalysis and the neurosciences compared. *International Journal of Psychoanalysis, 96*: 293–318.

Freud, S. (1895d [1893–95]) (with Breuer, J.). *Studies on Hysteria. Standard Edition, 2*.

Freud, S. (1900a). *The Interpretation of Dreams. Standard Edition*, 4–5.

Freud, S. (1911c [1910]). Psycho-analytic notes on an autobiographical account of a case of paranoia. *Standard Edition, 12*: 3–82.

Freud, S. (1914a). Fausse reconnaissance ("déjà raconté") in psycho-analytic treatment. *Standard Edition, 13*: 199–207.

Freud, S. (1914g). Remembering, repeating and working-through (Further recommendations on the technique of psycho-analysis). *Standard Edition, 12*: 147–156.

Freud, S. (1916–17). *Introductory Lectures on Psycho-Analysis. Standard Edition*, 15–16.

Freud, S. (1917d [1915]). A metapsychological supplement to the theory of dreams. *Standard Edition, 14*: 217–235.

Freud, S. (1920g). *Beyond the Pleasure Principle. Standard Edition, 18*: 7–64.

Freud, S. (1925h). Negation. *Standard Edition, 19*: 235–240.

Freud, S. (1933a). *New Introductory Lectures on Psycho-Analysis. Standard Edition, 22*: 3–182.

Freud, S. (1937d). Constructions in analysis. *Standard Edition, 23*: 255–269.

Green, A. (1986a). The borderline concept. In: *On Private Madness* (pp. 60–83). London: Hogarth Press & The Institute of Psychoanalysis.

Green, A. (1986b). The dead mother. In: *On Private Madness* (pp. 142–173). London: Hogarth Press and The Institute of Psychoanalysis.

Green, A. (1995). *Propédeutique. La métapsychologie revisitée.* Seyssel: Champ Vallon.

Green, A. (1999). *The Work of the Negative.* London: Free Association Books.

Green, A. (2001). *Life Narcissism, Death Narcissism.* London: Free Association Books.

Green, A. (2002). *Idées directrices pour une psychanalyse contemporaine.* Paris: Presses Universitaires de France.

Green, A. (2005a). *Key Ideas for a Contemporary Psychoanalysis: Misrecognition and Recognition of the Unconscious*, trans. A. Weller. London: Routledge.

Green, A. (2005b). Negation. In: R. J. Perelberg (Ed.), *Freud: A Modern Reader*. London: Whurr.

Grinberg, L. (1962). On a specific aspect of countertransference due to the patient's projective identification. *International Journal of Psychoanalysis, 43*: 436.

Heimann, P. (1950). On counter-transference. *International Journal of Psychoanalysis, 31*: 81–84.

Joseph, B. (1985). Transference: The total situation. *International Journal of Psychoanalysis, 66*: 447–454.

King, P. (1978). Affective response of the analyst to the patient's communications. *International Journal of Psychoanalysis, 59*: 329–334.

Kohon, G. (2000). Dreams, symbolic impoverishment and the question of the other. In: R. J. Perelberg (Ed.), *Dreaming and Thinking* (pp. 73–90). London: Karnac.

Kohon, G. (2010). Identification primaire et imago maternelle. In: *Libres cahiers pour la psychanalyse, No. 23: Transfert d'amours* (pp. 11–27). Paris: Editions In Press, 2011.

Kristeva, J. (1996). *Time and Sense: Proust and the Experience of Literature.* New York: Columbia University Press.

Lewin, B. D. (1948). Inferences from the dream screen. *International Journal of Psychoanalysis, 29*: 224–231.

Lorca, F. G. (1987). *Blood Wedding.* London: Methuen.

Perelberg, R. J. (1995). A core phantasy in violence. *International Journal of Psychoanalysis, 76*: 1215–1231.

Perelberg, R. J. (1998). "To be or not to be—here": A woman's denial of time and memory. In: J. Leff & R. J. Perelberg (Eds.), *Female Experience: Three Generations of Women on Work with Women* (pp. 60–76). London: Routledge.

Perelberg, R. J. (1999a). The interplay of identifications: Violence, hysteria and the repudiation of femininity. In: G. Kohon (Ed.), *The Dead Mother: The Work of André Green* (pp. 175–194). London: Routledge.

Perelberg, R. J. (1999b). The interplay between identifications and identity in the analysis of a violent young man. *International Journal of Psychoanalysis, 80*: 31–45.

Perelberg, R. J. (2000). The oracle in dreams: The past and the future in the present. In: R. J. Perelberg (Ed.), *Dreaming and Thinking* (pp. 109–128). London: Karnac.

Perelberg, R. J. (2003). Full and empty spaces in the analytic process. *International Journal of Psychoanalysis, 84*: 579–592.

Perelberg, R. J. (2006). The Controversial Discussions and *après-coup*. *International Journal of Psychoanalysis, 87*: 1199–1220.

Perelberg, R. J. (2007). Space and time in psychoanalytic listening. *International Journal of Psychoanalysis, 88*: 1473–1490.

Perelberg, R. J. (2008). *Time, Space and Phantasy.* London: Routledge.

Perelberg, R. J. (2011). "A father is being beaten": Constructions in the analysis of some male patients. *International Journal of Psychoanalysis, 92*: 97–116.

Perelberg, R. J. (2015a). Glossary. In: *Murdered Father, Dead Father: Revisiting the Oedipus Complex*. London: Routledge.

Perelberg, R. J. (2015b). On excess, trauma and helplessness: Repetitions and transformations. *International Journal of Psychoanalysis, 96*: 1453–1496.

Pirlot, G., & Cupa, D. (2012). *André Green. Les Grands concepts psychanalytiques*. Paris: Presses Universitaires de France.

Racker, H. (1968). *Transference and Countertransference*. London: Hogarth Press; new edition, London: Karnac, 1982.

Rolland, J. C. (2015). *Quatre essais sur la vie de l'âme*. Paris: Gallimard.

Sandler, J. (1976). Countertransference and role responsiveness. *International Review of Psycho-Analysis, 3*: 43–47.

Segal, H. (1957). Notes on symbol formation. *International Journal of Psychoanalysis, 38*: 391–397.

Segal, H. (1977). Countertransference. In: *The Work of Hanna Segal: A Kleinian Approach to Clinical Practice*. London: Karnac, 1986.

Spillius, E. B. (1992). Clinical experiences of projective identification. In: *Clinical Lectures on Klein and Bion* (pp. 57–70), ed. R. Anderson. London: Routledge.

Urribarri, F. (2005). Le Cadre de la representation dans la psychanalyse contemporaine. In: F. Richard & F. Urribarri (Eds.), *Autour de l'oeuvre d'André Green* (pp. 201–216). Paris: Presses Universitaires de France.

Urribarri, F. (2013). *Dialoguer avec André Green*. Paris: Éditions d'Ithaque.

Williams, P. (2004). Incorporation of an invasive object. *International Journal of Psychoanalysis, 85*: 1333–1348.

Winnicott, D. W. (1971). *Playing and Reality*. London: Tavistock Publications.

CHAPTER THREE

Troubled bodies: hypochondria, transformation, and the work of the negative

Jed Sekoff

I want to call upon a story about Green, whose work is especially poised to help with the complexities of the topic at hand. He had come to San Francisco to deliver a paper—it was difficult; and I conducted a public interview and discussion—he was charming. During a break I told him the following anecdote:

I had recently been to an exhibition of the work of Eva Hesse and my daughter, a bit of an artist herself, all nine years old of her, came along.[1]

I watched Lucia out of the corner of my eye, and as was her wont, she stood for a long while before certain pieces, quite still, intent. After a bit she came up to me and pronounced, "This is someone hanging on the edge of life and death."

That was one of those moments when you wonder whether your child . . . well, whether they are your child. Now it was I who stood still for a while, pausing on what had transpired. In the next room, there was some biographical information. Hesse, a Jewish, German-born American artist whose family fled the Nazis in 1938, developed a formidable body of work, only to die from a brain tumour at age 34. Doing some rough math, it seemed that some of the pieces Lucia was viewing may have been completed while Hesse was suffering from her cancer.

I subsequently learned that Hesse had escaped Germany on a *Kindertransport*, separated from her parents at age two for six months. Her family moved on to New York, her parents divorced, and one year after the war's end her mother committed suicide.

Now, this is the kind of uncanny story that usually has me fleeing in the other direction. Surely coincidence or an undetected source of knowledge will suffice as explanation. Still, if only for the sake of an interesting lunch, I posed the question: did Lucia actually "read" that Hesse was hanging between life and death? Had she entered into some unconscious alignment with the psychic envelope of the work?

After hearing me out, Green paused and, with more than a hint of dramatic effect, remarked, "The only surprise, is that you are surprised."

Well, yes. Yet, what actually did he mean? Was Green saying something along the lines of . . . and I'll need you to forgive my putting words into his mouth . . . "Naturally, of course. How could you forget the force of the unconscious? Its deep grammar, its occupation of the spaces between body and mind, between one subject and another, its elusive and yet palpable properties. Do we not see such resonances all around us, in each piece of myth, art, literature, or, God forbid, politics?" On the other hand, perhaps I was simply the unsuspecting recipient of his droll wit.

Regardless, I'll take the "surprised that you are surprised" as a gift for my discussion—though good sense should make me hesitate, given that the anecdote points in exactly the opposite direction of the hypochondriacal. If we accept the story of an unconscious communication between artist, artwork, and audience, we must accept the presence of a robust, if enigmatic, link between body, mind, and other: a link that must be fluid, undaunted by boundaries or barriers, and capable of a representability that encompasses both the imaginary and the real.

Hypochondriasis, on the other hand, runs in terror from the abyss of the Real, hijacks the Imaginary for its own anxious purposes, and resists the transformation of presentation into representation. Indeed, those with hypochondria face a seemingly unbridgeable gap between the body and the mind, the negative of what Winnicott called "indwelling" (1966, p. 515). We find in the frightened dislocation of hypochondria a psyche allergic to its own embodied self.

Hypochondria is an almost instantly recognisable aspect of all of our lives. As the great anatomist William Osler noted: "the desire to take medicine is perhaps the greatest feature that distinguishes man from animals" (in Cushing, 1956, p. 342). Once referred to as "The English Malady",[2] our troubled bodies trouble even those of us who live beyond these shores. Even so, hypochondria as a concept seems to have lost its pride of place. Psychosomatic phenomena, panic disorders, eating disorders, somatic delusions, body dysmorphias, those Japanese boys who won't leave their apartments—all refer to more contemporary renderings of mind–body problems.

How to sort all this through?

For the moment, I'll propose that a distinction be drawn between processes of *hypochondriacal retreat* and those of *psychosomatic collapse*. In some ways this is a matter of degree of disturbance—neurotic worry (hypochondriacal retreat) is not the same as psychotic delusion (which is often a last-ditch defence against psychosomatic collapse). Contrary to other mind–body conditions, the searing radical doubt of hypochondria—intensely painful, uniquely frightening as it is—does not in fact threaten the fabric of the psychic envelope. The mind has not evaporated, or buckled into the soma—indeed, it remains all too intact. Sadly, this is a reassurance that the hypochondriacal can never trust.

The work of the negative

In one of his few direct comments on hypochondria, Green (1999, p. 174) proposes that a "negativising" of sensations linked to the body and to the affects may take place under certain conditions, which he somewhat vaguely describes as a link to a background of negative hallucination. We might make progress with this by following Green's fundamental insight that the negative may function as an *unbinding of representation,* as well as a *template for representability.*

As the negative provides a framing structure (Perelberg, chapter 2) as well as a demolition, disruptions in this "double process" will do violence to the balance between perceptions of the body and those of thought. Somewhere in this imbalance, a hypochondriacal regime takes hold. These impingements may be traced back to the origins of the framing structure (Green, 1999; see also chapter 2), where impingements of neglect or "ever-presence" distort the formation of a "present absence"—Winnicott wrote of the necessity of "alive neglect" (1949, p. 245). In these deformations the work of the negative turns towards its darkest palette, the menacing shadows of a feared somatic collapse.

In Green's brief take, an enigmatic phrase occurs—a matter of translation perhaps—but the text refers to "hypochondria or certain passionate manifestations" (Green, 1999, p. 174). What are these "passionate manifestations"? Perhaps a clue exists when Green distilled his reflection on *the work of the negative* into the following sentence:

> The work of the negative comes down to one question: faced with the destruction which threatens everything, can a way be found for desire to live and love? [Green, 2005, p. 220]

Is this not the hypochondriacal question?

For the subject in the throes of hypochondria, the world of the living beckons, love and desire are known and enjoyed, and yet, painfully, maddeningly, these connections may be severed without a moment's notice. Why the expulsion? Paradoxically, the world is rejected *because its destruction cannot be tolerated.* "Passionate manifestations"—the pulse of an engaged life with all of its destructive currents—are seen as a persecutory threat, and the subject's most ardent attentions are consigned to the beating of their own heart.

And this takes me to the core of my argument. Hypochondria is, above all else, an unconscious strategy of containment whose aim is to ensure that the subject will not enter the pulse of the world, principally because they dare *not fall prey to unbidden and unwanted transformation.* In their desperate wish to somehow guarantee continuity, plenitude, and safe haven, the hypochondriacal cast of mind becomes a minefield of refusals.

We will have to see whether the argument holds, but, for the moment, I want to think with you about The Cure—the band, not the therapeutic aim. Well, actually, a little bit of both.

Sam

Sam enters the room, in something like the twelfth year of our analytic work, and, before lying down, he turns and shows me a video on his mobile phone of his one-year-old daughter saying "da–da" for the first time. I'm struck by how calm he seems, how happy—so far from the trembling, disheartened young man on the edge of failing university when we first met. The shared video seemed to me less an "acting-in" than a first association to whatever state he had brought us that day.

> He lies down and announces: "Things are going well ... good ... been less focused on getting fired ... but also I've been walking around worried about having a heart attack."
>
> It turns out he had had some "chest pain" ... so much so, he saw a physician, who diagnosed muscle strain. Nevertheless, "I can't get it out of my head." He began reading about heart attacks online and recited his symptoms: "Chest pain, pain in the arms, trouble breathing, having a feeling of impending doom."
>
> I say: "I think you can check the last one off your list ... don't think you need a heart attack to feel impending doom."
>
> S [laughs]: "True, true ... but ... early this week, I was reading about it online, and I fainted ... I just collapsed to the floor. C (his wife) was frightened, she said I was frozen for moment, my mouth open. When I came to, I was humming."
>
> Me [a bit quickly]: "What song?"
>
> S [confused]: "WHAT? ... what song ... um ... um ... not sure. ... Oh, 'Let's Go to Bed', by The Cure [1982]"
>
> Me: "The 'Cure'."
>
> S: "Oh, come on ... do you really think this has some unconscious meaning? That the song ... the humming [he emphasises the distinction from a song] ... in my head points to something?"
>
> [I'm quiet.]

S: "Well, I haven't heard it in years . . . but I know the words, most of them: 'Let me take your hands. I'm shaking like milk, turning, turning blue. Fires outside in the sky look as perfect as cats, and I don't feel, if you don't, and I don't want it, if you don't. Stay alive, but stay the same—it's a stupid game.'"

As he recites the lyrics, I find that the colours stand out in my mind, which I name: milky-white and trouble-breathing blue. I recall his father's heart trouble. That he often worries that his cat may die. I also think of when, as a young boy, he clung so tightly to the leg of his mother he would have to be pried loose.

S: "Okay . . . What are you saying?"

Me: "I was thinking more about what you were singing."

He seems annoyed, but then continues.

S: "I used to like the part in the song about 'look as perfect as cats'. Not sure what I think [emphasising the 'I'] about the shaking milk." [Then, almost to himself] "I don't feel if you don't."

Suddenly, he becomes combative. [And I realise how absent this has been.]

S: "And if I dropped dead tomorrow from a heart attack, would you say: 'Oh, I was wrong, there is no unconscious!'"

And I replied, in turn,

Me: "Yes, that's what I would say . . . I'd say, 'Poor guy. Very upsetting, but I guess there is no unconscious, so I got my own troubles'."

[He laughs, somewhat begrudgingly.]

"Then again, I might think you really went pretty far to interrupt feeling better. That things moving on in life can be very threatening. That you might be very worried about showing me how much pleasure you have in being a father, of being less worried in life."

S: "You know G [his daughter] has started to wean . . . I guess that means cow's milk from here out . . . [laughs] . . . . 'Da Da' not her first words, her first were 'hi' and 'bye'. She is very into waving goodbye now. She also says 'dada work', when I leave the room."

Me: "Things come and go. People come and go. They don't always stay the same. Staying alive doesn't depend on it . . . Isn't that the Cure's interpretation?"

S: "Guess so, yes. She has so many words."

He then sings part of the song for me, as the session ends.

Now, this represents a symptomatic episode, not a life in the thrall of hypochondriacal anxiety. As such, we can only glean a few bare points:

As the song proclaims: "Stay alive, but stay the same." It turns out that it may be very hard to watch your child turn you into a father, or your work give you success, or your wife shower you with love—especially hard when "hi" and "bye" have not yet taken hold in your own vocabulary. Sam tells himself that chests should not have pangs, mummies' legs should never move, daddies should never grow old, and milk should be neither stirred nor shaken, just ever-flowing. Time is not to enter the never-ending nursery.

Twin phantasies

Sam offers material to illustrate what I have found to be two organising phantasies of hypochondria: *the phantasy of the neutral body* and *the phantasy of the immutable other*. These twin phantasies form a bulwark against *entering time* and *re-shaping psychic space*. A "neutral body" is a body without vagaries or oscillations, immune to unauthorised sensations, and resistant to any evidence of time's passage. An "immutable other" will never go away, never change, never abandon—an immortal denizen of a frozen internal world. [3]

Ironically, for the hypochondriacal everything is in motion. The body rumbles, creaks, and sometimes quakes. So many currents to stir an anxious vigilance, for our bodies are not the "big sagacity" that Nietzsche prized over "ego"[4] but, on the contrary, a source of mystery, terror, and confusion. What is your pulse saying? Is that your pancreas calling? Try describing a pain to your physician and notice the impoverished vocabulary that sputters forth. The inner recesses of our soma rarely speak above a whisper, and when they do—watch out, trouble is on the horizon.

I want to pause for a moment and ask a question. What happens when an actual illness befalls the hypochondriacal, or the loss of a loved one interrupts their retreat? More often than not, the fearful subject turns calm or brave, helplessness gives way to resourcefulness, and dread melts into stoic resolve.

To take one example: an analysand who was under constant hypochondriacal siege was thrust by acute abdominal pain into an emergency-room visit. The pain itself seemed to have arisen when the analysis exposed fault lines in the idolisation of her mother, provoking a psychosomatic collapse—that is, a form of representational collapse. No source was found for the pain, which quickly subsided.

However, the MRI that was conducted did hold one shocking finding . . . all the organs in her abdomen were reversed!—a condition that, her sensitive doctor announced, "could kill you at any time". In fact, he was "amazed" that she had survived childhood. My own thought was that I would be amazed if the analysis would survive this physician.

Instead, thoughts about this condition hardly arose again in the following years. Similarly, tortuous fears about the health of her mother and husband were met head-on when they each required crisis hospitalisations. Perhaps the only surprise is that I was surprised. The hypochondriacal body is phantasmatic, phantasies deployed for dynamic purpose. The "actual" body is "recruited" for these purposes, but, paradoxically, the "realness" of a condition may disqualify or impinge upon its value as a reservoir for doubt, masochistic enthrallment, or anxious elaboration. This is a difficult point to make, but clinically it appears that a symbolic diagnosis or a crisis in the "real" *threads the subject back into time*, dissolving—for a time—the body's utility as the leading character in the unconscious drama of refusal and retreat.

Sam, by the way, early in our time together, had a cancer diagnosis, unusual for someone his age. He was treated successfully and considered cured, though he required semi-annual checkups that involved a fair amount of discomfort. Again, fears about recurrence or memories of his procedure were rarely discernible.

The hollowing

I want to raise what might also be a surprising finding. For the hypochondriacal, the object—so essential and central to their project—has, in fact, few anchors in their internal world. On the one hand, the object is leaned upon, feted, always kept in sight—nothing may happen to it, it must be protected at all costs. And yet, at the very same time, the other is blighted by what Green termed "objectal disqualification" or "disobjectalising" (1999, p. 108).

A desperately needed object is a desperately feared object. Its power must be kept at bay. If you ask, you may be told that the face or image of the other is vague or missing—a confession that is felt as bizarre, shameful, or crazy. I have come to think of this as a *"hollowing out of the object"*, which leaves *the form* of the other as a site of attachment, while *the substance* or *specificity* of the other is erased or rendered useless.[5]

Still, no one can do without an other, and this gives rise to a constant pressure to "fabricate" the object, to be the sole guardian of the object's life and death. This house of cards continually collapses, only to be feverishly reconstituted before buckling once again, in a seemingly perpetual cycle.

Two ancillary points: on the one hand, it is important to repeat a complex amendment—namely, that for Green it is not the object per se that is of import but, rather, an "objectalising" transformative process. To "fabricate" an object is to disrupt the complex dialectic that establishes the arc between drive and structure, presentation and representation, subject and other. No structural sustenance is found through fabricated, or "patched" objects (Green, 1986, p. 152). In such a de-stabilised terrain, ideas, sensations, and impulses easily become infectious agents, and the world is always shadowed by unbound contagion.

At the same time (and from an opposite direction), it seems that the concrete, palpable experience *of* and *with* the parental body(ies) establishes the somatic ground of every subject. If these bodily experiences cannot be specifically and substantively visualised, proprioceptively recalled, or affectively invested (with idiosyncratic details, along with particular pleasures in particular parts), a grave impoverishment in the subject's own somatic stability occurs. The hollow of the object becomes a hole, soon enough filled with threat and dread.

Sexuality drive

I am aware that I have directed my focus here on the fate of subject–object relations, while largely leaving aside—what no homage to Green should do—a discussion of sexuality and the drives. It is almost a truism to say that for the neurotic, their symptoms *are* their sex, and so it seems in hypochondria. Masochism—or masoch*isms*, as Green reminds us—offers a channel for the drive to find its bitter satisfactions. From another angle, we find what Green called the heightened sexual "conflagration" of an Oedipus who not only sleeps with his mother but must resuscitate her again and again (1986, p. 159).

Still, masochism or oedipal catastrophe do not give us a complete picture. It is not so much the "narcissisation of suffering" that describes the sexual economy here but, rather, a heightening of all sensations related to the object. The drives are enlisted in a "libidinal co-excitation" that sensually secures the phantasy of the immutable other. However, a body primed to feel a fever pitch of sensuality violates the principle of the "neutral body". Pleasure, then, is always a guilty pleasure, and a price must be exacted. The fear of one's demise is that payment plus interest.

To put this another way: the aliveness of the sexual proves both a lure and a hazard to the hypochondriacal subject. The sexual binds the subject to the other, offering assurance that their link will never be broken, that mourning will always be deferred. Auto-erotic phantasy and sexual encounter may be highly valued, a source of profound satisfaction. Yet, once again, satisfaction gives way to despair, as the momentary ascendency of Eros cannot quiet the demand that time, loss, and death be expelled from paradise.

In the midst of this wrenching struggle between life and death, sexuality and drive are not so much banished as deferred. Thought becomes the domain of the erotic—a deferral that Green also identifies in the dead mother complex. A compulsion to imagine and a compulsion to think (1986, p. 152) mask the psychic holes left by extruded satisfactions and displaced objects. Worse, this intense mental activity feeds the radical doubt of hypochondria and lays the basis for another set of anxieties—namely, that the desperately valued torrent of thought will itself collapse.

Terror of losing one's mind is concretised in fears of failing memory, thinning vocabulary, confusional episodes, or mental collapse. Many patients report a panic that they will suddenly lose consciousness, stop speaking, or become blank, completely unable to think. Mental hypochondria is yet another subset of the hypochondriacal arsenal of worry and woe. For some, it is the most horrific of symptoms: after all, sick bodies can be ministered to—if reached in the nick of time!—while a faltering mind jeopardises the very essence of our sense of being.

It has been my observation that almost without exception patients of a certain age (let's say all those past 50)[6] voice grave concerns about dementia or Alzheimer's. Would it be going too far to claim that such anxieties, rooted in the realities of aging as they clearly are, could nevertheless be seen as kin to the hypochondriacal demand for neutral bodies and unalterable objects? Perhaps as we age, we inherently fall under the sway of the twin phantasies of hyphochondria—each of us, in different measure, stoic and hysteric alike, raging silently—and symptomatically—against the dying of the light.

Analytic process

And what might we say of the hypochondriacal subject, object, and desire as they make their appearance in the analytic field?

Turning back to my work with Sam, I seem to be functioning as both *lure* and *pivot*—a seducer who tempts the patient to emerge from his adhesive and claustrophobic state, all the while turning towards a representational rather than presentational world. It seems imperative that the hypochondriacal find a fluid, robust, and desirous analytic object; one capable of eluding sequestration, while pressing a demand for response.

Such *press*—let's call it *play* (in the deepest Winnicottian sense)—might be understood as a species of what Green termed "arborescence" (Green, 2002), the radiating associative nature of mind: a movement from root to branch to stem to leaf, outward and inward and round again. As Green makes clear, our radial representational processes always emerge within a complex and contested dialectic. Only a technique alive to this fullness of the arborescent will suffice.

And what might the labours of the analytic couple bring forth? To break the phantasmagoric stasis of the neutral body and the immutable other, the hypochondriacal subject must brave death and contemplate murder. The symmetrical equation of individuation with obliteration must be cast aside, and with that comes the agreement that both subject and object will die—though "perhaps not just yet". I admit that "not just yet" is a weak invitation, but such are the meagre wares of our craft.

Transformation will also depend upon withstanding the paradoxical overwhelm of actually inhabiting a body, rather than controlling (or being controlled by) a corporeal phantom. Movement must displace stillness, contact must replace encapsulation, and time must be entered once more.

In closing

To conclude, I take the hypochondriacal to be an essential human condition, an unavoidable unconscious position that the subject must encounter to fully enter a realm of meaning. Hypochondria expresses our most radical doubt, exposes our deepest wishes to refuse time and transformation, and yet still offers evidence of our dogged desire to inhabit a world of love, meaning, and connection.

As Green has shown us, it is only if we accept the turbulent work of the negative that we may find the means to live and love. And so, too, it is only if we traverse the terrors of our bodily imagination that we may find the psychic resources to brave our all too perilous fate.[7]

Notes

1. You can get a rough idea of the exhibition from the San Francisco Museum of Modern Art website [https://www.sfmoma.org/artist/Eva_Hesse], with further images on the Hauser & Wirth website [http://www.hauserwirth.com/artists/34/eva-hesse/images-clips].

2. In 1734 George Cheyne wrote a rather long, yet entertaining response to the accusation of English hypochondria. I will risk quoting it at length: "The title for this treatise, is a reproach universally thrown on this island by foreigners, and all our neighbours on the continent, by whom nervous distempers, spleen, vapours, and lowness of spirits, are, in derision, call'd the English Malady. And I wish there were not so good grounds for this reflection. The moisture of our air, the variableness of our weather . . . the rankness and fertility of our soil, the richness . . . of our food, the wealth and abundance of the inhabitants . . . the inactivity and sedentary occupations of the better sort (among whom this evil mostly rages) and the humour of living in great, populous, and . . . unhealthy towns, have brought forth a class and set of distempers, with atrocious and frightful symptoms, scarce known to our ancestors, and never rising to such fatal heights, nor afflicting such numbers in any other known nation. These nervous disorders being computed to make almost one third of the complaints of the people of condition in England."

3. I take "entering time" and "re-shaping psychic space" to be versions of Green's conception of the "objectalising function". The latter is not simply a means of relating to an object (internal or external) but a transformative process that gives meaningful investment to various psychic structures—as if they were objects (i.e. the ego). The twin phantasies of hypochondria would enact then a "withdrawal of investment", or a "disobjectalising" (see Green, 1999, pp. 85–86).

4. "Ego, sayest thou, and art proud of that work. But the greater thing-in which thou art unwilling to believe-is thy body with its big sagacity; it saith not 'ego', but doeth it" (Nietzsche, 1891, p. 30).

5. This finding of the value of an object's form rather than its substance echoes Green's observation that in the analysis of the "dead mother", the analysis is more cathected than the analyst (1986, p. 161).

6. The comedian and writer Steve Martin (1998) has described what it is like to turn 50: "1. Place your car keys in your right hand. 2. With your left hand, call a friend and confirm a lunch or dinner date. 3. Hang up the phone. 4. Pick up your keys, walk outside, now find your keys."

7. I find an echo of this sentiments in Yeats' poem, "The Circus Animal's Desertion" (1933): "I must lie down where all the ladders start. / In the foul rag and bone shop of the heart." André Green offers a parallel diagnosis of the wellspring of rag and bone.

References

Cheyne, G. (1734). *The English Malady or, a Treatise of Nervous Diseases of all Kinds; as Spleen, Vapours, Lowness of Spirits, Hypochondriachal, and Hysterical Distempers, Etc.* Available at: https://archive.org/details/englishmaladyort00cheyuoft

Cushing, H. (1956). *The Life of Sir William Osler.* Oxford: Oxford University Press.

Green, A. (1986). The dead mother. In: *On Private Madness* (pp. 142–173). London: Hogarth Press & The Institute of Psychoanalysis.

Green, A. (1999). *The Work of the Negative.* London: Free Association Books.

Green, A. (2002). *Time in Psychoanalysis.* London: Free Association Books.

Green, A. (2005). *Key Ideas for a Contemporary Psychoanalysis: Misrecognition and Recognition of the Unconscious,* trans. A. Weller. London: Routledge.

Martin, S. (1998). Changes in the memory after fifty. *The New Yorker,* 19 January.

Nietzsche, F. (1891). *Thus Spake Zarathustra.* Ware: Wordsworth Editions, 1997.

Winnicott, D. W. (1949). Mind and its relation to the psyche-soma. In: *Through Paediatrics to Psychoanalysis* (pp. 243–254). London: Hogarth Press, 1975; reprinted London: Karnac, 1984.

Winnicott, D. W. (1966). Psychosomatic illness in its positive and negative aspects. *International Journal of Psychoanalysis, 47:* 510–516.

Yeats, W. B. (1990). *The Collected Poems of W. B. Yeats.* London: Picador.

CHAPTER FOUR

Some thoughts on the negative in the work of Eduardo Chillida

Gregorio Kohon

In this chapter I consider the negative in the work of Eduardo Chillida and draw on the explorations contained in my book, *Reflections on the Aesthetic Experience: Psychoanalysis and the Uncanny* (Kohon, 2016). In it, I refer to the catalogue of the exhibition of Joshua Neustein's work at the Israel Museum in Jerusalem in 2012, where Meira Perry-Lehman (the curator of the exhibition) described how the artist proceeded with his work. First, Neustein scribbled a drawing on a sheet of paper; he then erased some of the drawn lines, creating a sharp-edged square. What was left of the original drawing, including the erased lines, echoed two operations: the act of drawing and the act of erasing. Neustein then collected the residue and affixed it to the bottom of the sheet, upholding its presence.

The exhibition displayed a series of such "erased drawings"—a description that expresses a logical contradiction, as the drawings were created through erasing: the rubbing out of what had been drawn *made* the drawing possible. As I argued in my book,

> Normally, a picture does not exist before it is created; it is given existence through the determined action of drawing or painting. Where there was "nothing", now there is "something". How-

ever, in the case of the "erased drawings", the final form—the
exhibited product hanging on the wall—materialised through
the negative: something could now be seen, but not simply
because it was "invisible" before. Neustein's pictures come
into being only because, paradoxically, they are erased. This
is accomplished not through an epistemological change (let us
say, a change in the quality of the object itself) but through a
profound change in the symbolic status of the object. [Kohon,
2016, p. 139]

Something comparable takes place in the aesthetic experience of
modern sculpture, where questions of interior and exterior, solid
and void, weight and weightlessness, and the issues of time and
space have become fundamental at the moment of their creation—
and, later, in the consequent perception, appreciation, and understanding of the works. Sculptures are no longer solid objects with
a symbolic role on a pedestal surrounded by space, like the ancient
Greek sculptures. The viewer is now invited to move around,
sometimes on, in, or through the sculptures: emptiness forms part
of their structure. Whether placed in a museum or situated in an
outside space and open landscape, the works created make the
subject participate through anticipation, memory, and attention.

This is clearly illustrated in the work of Richard Serra. The
two sculptures *Junction* (2011) and *Cycle* (2010), which he presented at the Gagosian Gallery, in New York, in 2012, followed the
same inspiration as his work at the Bilbao Guggenheim (Kohon,
2016).

Cycle is formed by two great curved pieces of steel meeting in an
apparently single opening. One single opening turns into two: one
opening leads into a large, empty, round room; the other follows a
path of narrow walls where coloured sands and ocean waves may
be imagined. There are different openings confronting the visitor,
who has to make a choice, each opening leading to a different
exit. One is permanently tempted to re-enter the sculpture from
different places, to walk around, going in and out several times,
experiencing the sculpture from different angles and in its different forms. These are sculptures to be "walked": static observation
is not possible. At every step, the visitor is led to the creation of
new meanings. Here there is an invitation from the artist to be a
participant—but this is only achieved in Serra's sculptures through

the experience of negative space. The negative—establishing meaning. These sculptures add further complexity to the ideas originally developed in the series, "The Matter of Time", at the Guggenheim (Kohon, 2016).

Serra pointed out in an interview that it was an *"interval* of choice" that made the sculptures particularly interesting. This moment of the interval, of having to make a choice, disrupts one's thoughts: time is suspended (Serra, in Goldstein, 2011). While we occupy the space of the sculptures, walking around and through them, time does not follow a continuity: everything—the interval of choice, breaking the sequence, the cadence of the visitor's movements—creates a disorienting effect. There appears to be a multiplicity of "realities" in that space and that time. It is a moment of depersonalisation and loss—loss, void, absence. The challenge lies in experiencing the intervals of time, creating different spaces. This is something that closely resembles André Green's concept of a "tree of time", a tree-like structure of time (2002, p. 162).

Green conceived this as a network of simultaneously divergent forces and paths that nevertheless operate together, but without ever becoming an absolute unity. Events cannot therefore be explained as simple cause-and-effect development; they do not end at a given chronological point: they continue to exist while staying the same and while going on transforming themselves. There is timelessness in the unconscious—but this does not mean that there is no temporality. No two readings of any particular event are ever exactly the same: with each reading we effectively change the events that have already happened during our first reading. With each further perception, appraisal, and interpretation, the event changes in meaning, the negative forming an indissoluble part of it.

As also argued in my 2016 book, the negative is a fundamental theoretical tenet in psychoanalysis, best represented by André Green's concept of the *work of the negative* (1997, 1999). According to Green, the presence of the negative is to be found in Freud's concept of the unconscious itself, where the prefix *un–* already provides a clear reference to it. In Freudian theory, there is no clinical or theoretical concept that does not relate to the unconscious and turn thus to the negative. According to Green, the work of the negative brings together ". . . the aspects inherent to the most general psychic activity" common to all human beings (1999, p. 12).

There is a paradoxical quality in the negative; it represents a dual mode of thinking. Negation will never be completely successful; the splitting of the ego will allow for knowing and not knowing at one and the same time; repression will produce symptoms and dreams, thus revealing what has been kept hidden (Kohon, 1999). The work of the negative is infused with this fundamental dual mode, which is part of the legacy inherited by Green (via Jacques Lacan and Alexandre Kojève) from Hegel and his thoughts concerning dialectics.

The importance of Green's concept can be seen in the work of the Spanish sculptor Eduardo Chillida, who died in 2002, aged 78. From very early on in his career, Chillida had many international admirers and received special recognition, winning all major international prizes. Martin Heidegger believed that Chillida's sculptures were a defiance and a challenge to the scientific, quantifiable discourse on time (Heidegger, 1969). Another philosopher, Gaston Bachelard, wrote the essay, "The Cosmos of Fire", for the catalogue of Chillida's exhibition at the Maeght Gallery (Bachelard, 1956). He thought that Chillida had the ability to reveal the "realities of air" through sculptures made of iron; this represented for him a great dream of primitive humanity. Emil Cioran, the Romanian philosopher and essayist, was very pleased to have Chillida's illustrations for a special, exclusive edition of one of his books (Cioran, 1983). Another admirer was the Mexican poet and 1990 winner of the Nobel Prize in Literature, Octavio Paz, who spoke of Chillida's work as verging "at one extreme, on a cruel sexuality, and at the other on a winged elegance", adding that, in his sculptures, "iron says wind, wood says song, alabaster says light—but all say the same thing: space" (Paz, 1967).

Chillida combined sculptural forms and environmental spaces to produce extraordinary urban landscapes. He thought of his sculptures as a "rebellion against gravity", where there is a dialectic between the empty and full space, between movement and static tension. *Elogio del Horizonte,* for example, standing on the top of the hill of Santa Catalina, near Gijón, in the Bay of Biscay, and facing the Cantabrian Sea, is a gigantic, monumental work. It was constructed of reinforced concrete—perhaps the least "aesthetic" material imaginable (Figure 4.1).

FIGURE 4.1.   *Elogio del Horizonte IV*, 1989.
Image provided by Banco de Imágenes de VEGAP.

Nevertheless, it is the sea, the wind, the ground that become the main aspect of the work. Looking at it, one cannot but feel a mixture of admiration and reverence and be touched and even inspired by such a creation. If one stands in the middle of the sculpture, inside the huge empty space created by the concrete pillars, the sound of the sea and the wind seems to be amplified, developing into a magnificent presence in one's mind.

What seems to be "missing" in the sculptures is what *creates* the space, bringing forward what does not belong to the actual physical structure. According to Chillida, there is a rebellion against gravity in his creations: a particular dialectic is created between the voids, which form an indissoluble part of the sculpture, and the full presence and weight of the material used in the work.

Perhaps the most illustrative creation of this dialectic is *Peine del Viento*, Chillida's own favourite creation (Figure 4.2). For many critics, it is his masterpiece. Standing at the foot of Mount Igeldo, *Peine del Viento* was installed in 1977. The three spectacular pieces of steel, each weighing 11 tons, are dramatically anchored three

FIGURE 4.2   *Peine del Viento XV* (Tres), 1976.
Image provided by Banco de Imágenes de VEGAP.

feet into the rock of the cliffs, at the western edge of the Bay of San Sebastian, surrounded by the waves of the sea. While *Elogio del Horizonte* was oriented towards the sky, *el Peine* is in a constant dialogue with the sea. Chillida claimed that these sculptures are not, as it were, "included" in a space that was already there. It is the work itself that creates the space, the surrounding landscape becoming part of the sculpture.

The three pieces can be imagined as claylike fingers or appendages, one reaching upward and two horizontal, which seem to yearn towards each other. For Chillida, the three different sculptures formed one integral work: he argued that the nearest two represent the past and the present, connected to and yet separated from each other. The future is defined by the vertical piece, at the furthest point from the viewer, pointing towards what is to come. However, the logic of this work of art appears to transcend the artist's own explanations. In fact, I would argue that the work evokes the unconscious experience of time, where past and present are determined not by a beginning of a life, let us say, but by the origin of a story.

Despite Chillida's description, the observer may not necessarily see the sculptural pieces as being inside time—that is, being determined by a chronological sequence, with a symbolic past, present, and future indicated by the three different pieces. There is a timelessness in the position they occupy, and yet this does not imply that they can exist outside time or be transcendent of it.

Somewhat paradoxically, this is not dissimilar to the way scientists understand the notion of time. When his great friend, Michele Besso, died, Albert Einstein wrote to Michele's sister: "People like us, who believe in physics, know that the distinction made between past, present and future is nothing more than a persistent, stubborn illusion" (quoted in Rovelli, 2014).

If it is true to say—as argued by Chillida—that there is no space in the artist's work that contains his creations, no spatial parameter that would determine a specific point of reference, similarly there is no single given past, present, or future moment that would define a particular time belonging to the work itself. The three sculptures, static against the tides, fixed into the rocks, are witness to the simultaneous moving away from an unknown and undefined origin, towards an equally unknown, uncertain future. The wind, the mist, the different lengths of the days at different times of the year, the eternal changing of the weather, the sounds, the fury of the storms—this is all that can be stated. We cannot live there, we can only dream about it.

Furthermore, and more relevantly, I would suggest that it is not a question of *what* symbolic meaning the three pieces contain or imply but *how*, when each wave is individually contemplated as part of the landscape surrounding the sculptures, meaning is created. The waves generate and give a meaning to the static sculpture through a process of repetition that is never the same. And here is the paradox: being different, *repetition can never be the same*—the waves come and go, each forever completely different from the previous ones. The memory of each wave, somewhat familiar to us, disappears with the immediate arrival of another, a completely unfamiliar, unknown one. The sense of repetition becomes uncanny: it comes to constitute a memory of a thing that has never happened before. It can be described, not so much as a form of remembering, but as a "negative form of forgetting" (Hillis Miller, 1982, p. 7).

In *The Tempest*, anticipating his daughter's wedding to the Prince of Naples, Prospero has staged a short entertainment, with spirits taking the parts of Roman gods. At a certain point, he declares:

> Our revels now are ended. These our actors,
> As I foretold you, were all spirits, and
> Are melted into air, into thin air:
> And like the baseless fabric of this vision,
> The cloud-capp'd tow'rs, the gorgeous palaces,
> The solemn temples, the great globe itself,
> Yea, all which it inherit, shall dissolve,
> And, like this insubstantial pageant faded,
> Leave not a rack behind. We are such stuff
> As dreams are made on; and our little life
> Is rounded with a sleep.
>
> *The Tempest* Act 4, Scene 1, ll. 148–158

The performance, Prospero claims, is simply an illusion; "all spirits" are bound, sooner or later, to melt into "thin air". The play is a metaphor for the world outside the theatre, equally fleeting; everything in that world will eventually crumble and "dissolve"; time will inexorably pass, leaving not even a "rack" behind. The performance is a play within Shakespeare's play; both are an illusion imbued in temporality, as is the world itself. People, we are told, are the "stuff" dreams are "made on". Prospero's "stuff" refers to the creation of an uncanny illusion, not to the object of our desires. The "great globe itself", which is where we exist, work, and love, is not ours to possess: in this scenario, the most familiar becomes utterly alien.

Works of literature and art open the possibility of experiencing multiple temporalities, both contradictory and uncanny—like the figures of a dream. Artistic creations, as indeed literary creations, are strange things, illusions, but so is science. Einstein's equation describing the curvature of time proved that indeed space curves. That's it: a "simple" equation. But, as Carlo Rovelli explains to us laymen: ' . . . here the magical richness of theory opens up into a phantasmagorical succession of predictions that resemble the delirious ravings of a madman, but which have all turned out to be true' (p. 7). Delirious, but true. Space is not the only thing that curves. We are told that time curves too. I do not understand it but I have to believe it: 'Einstein predicted that time passes more quickly high up than below, nearer to the Earth. This was measured and turned out to be the case. If a man who has lived at sea level meets up with a twin who has lived in the mountains, he will find that his sibling is slightly older than him' (p. 8). This is but a glimpse of reality—similar and comparable to the psychic reality as revealed by psychoanalysis. Our dreams are made on this same stuff, and so are our aesthetic experiences.

A patient tells me, 'My father was in my dream last night; it was my father, and, yet, I'm quite certain that it could have also been my friend Rob: he had his long, curly hair, the same North London Jewish accent . . . I always thought of Rob as a very sadistic kind of a guy . . .' This is the stuff that dreams are *made on*: an illusion of a similarity that exists only through the differences between one person (the father) and another (the friend). This is a "negative form of forgetting" (Hillis Miller, 1982), which becomes meaningful through a process of *après-coup*: the memory of the friend throws potential light on the forgetting of the father (see Perelberg, 2006, 2007, 2008). This is *in between* a remembering and a forgetting, something which defines the uncanny character of our dreams, the surreal sense of existence in which all human beings live.

Any temporal distinction in Chillida's creation constitutes superimposed interpretations based on the assumption of a linear understanding of time. Nevertheless, the work of art opens the possibility of multiple temporalities, eventually contradictory, like the figures of a dream. Artistic creations, as indeed literary creations, are strange things, illusions—but so is science.

Chillida's three sculptures (Figure 4.2) produce a moment of depersonalisation and loss: there is a multiplicity of possible, potential temporal and physical "realities" taking place. The three pieces constitute one single creation, but there is no coherent unity in this work of art.

I would argue that a similar use of space and time can be present and experienced in all forms of art and literature: the uncanny is not a feature of contemporary art alone. For example, looking at Vermeer's *Lady at the Virginals with a Gentleman*, we may notice a number of unfamiliar things in the familiarity of the scene, which inevitably produces a feeling of estrangement. There is a woman, of whom we see only her back, ostensibly having a music lesson with her music teacher—all rather normal, commonplace, mundane—and this is the usual interpretation of the painting. Everything seems chaste and understated. And yet, after the first minutes of contemplating the picture, we cannot completely relax into this normalised version of the painting; unwittingly, we resist this "normality". What makes us feel uncomfortable? Why is the identity of the lady, for example, hidden? Who is she? There is more here than meets the eye; doubts about our initial perception start creeping in.

The painter used a semi-precious stone, lapis lazuli, as colour; Vermeer had also laid an underpainting to achieve certain effects, a complete extravagance for the times! The initial simple beauty that we observed in the painting begins to convey something enigmatic and unsettling.

There is a cello on the floor, in rather a strange position, behind the lady. It is a music lesson, so why should there not be a cello on the floor? It makes sense. But the more I look at the painting, the less convinced I am: the effect produced in me is to make me curious and intrigued: I remain unsettled. The cello seems to represent something alien, as if it should not be there.

In the mid-seventeenth century, the cello was taken as a symbol of harmony in a couple—specifically marital harmony, but also sexual harmony. So, who is the man next to the lady? An innocent music teacher, as we initially thought? Or is he a lover? Or her husband? Or, much more interestingly, is he a music teacher (the "familiar") who is also her lover ("the alien", "the intruder")? Have we found the reason *why* the identity of the woman has to be hidden? Here there is the "in-between": on the one hand, the cool and chaste initial beauty of the picture; on the other, the discomfort of the observer. This area of the in-between becomes the playground where an imaginary passionate story of a clandestine love affair can be constructed and developed by the observer.

For a long time, the poet Elizabeth Bishop wished that someone would compare her poems to the paintings of Vermeer, and this was finally done by the poet and critic Randall Jarrell. In telling this story in his accomplished book on Bishop, Colm Tóibín describes the Dutch paintings as ". . . something made that is both real and filled with detail, but, in the play of light and shadow, in the placing of people and things, in the making of figures, it is also totally suggestive, without any of the suggestions being easy or obvious" (Tóibín, 2015, p. 23). Equally, the power of Bishop's poems come from somewhere in-between "what is said and what lies beneath . . ." (p. 23).

This is the world of poetry, a poetic world present in literature and in the arts, not a world created just by words, paint, wood, ceramic, or concrete, as they are used in the artists' creations, but by the silences, the emptiness, the voids that exist within, and in-between: a psychoanalytic world.

Conclusion

From a psychoanalytic point of view, the negotiations between "who I am" and its negative, "who I am *not*", are at the heart of the paradox of human subjectivity. Being familiar to myself, how can I recognise myself in what I am not? Or, alternatively, how can my own self be so *un*-familiar to me that I might not recognise it in a mirror or in a photograph? Perhaps we could have no better example of the complex dialectics involved in the process of identification and self-recognition (or misidentification and misrecognition) than the one given by Freud in a footnote in "The 'Uncanny'":

> I was sitting alone in my *wagon-lit* compartment when a more than usually violent jolt of the train swung back the door of the adjoining washing-cabinet, and an elderly gentleman in a dressing-gown and a travelling cap came in. I assumed that in leaving the washing-cabinet, which lay between the two compartments, he had taken the wrong direction and come into my compartment by mistake. Jumping up with the intention of putting him right, I at once realized to my dismay that the intruder was nothing but my own reflection in the looking-glass of the open door. [Freud, 1919h, p. 248]

The mirror stage offers the opportunity for a full identification, the first (perhaps) mythical moment when the subject can gain access to being a subject and can move away from primary narcissism. Nevertheless, being an illusion, this identification with an image in the mirror produces a double of the subject, turning into a source of alienation: being turns into not-being, the familiar becomes unfamiliar. For human beings, there is no escape from this imaginary identification: it is what it is.

De M'Uzan argues that, even though the statement, "I am me and not someone else", should be self-evident, there are no guarantees; this kind of certainty can crumble fairly easily. The original, primary, and confusing boundaries between me and not-me will continue as a psychic function for the rest of one's life (de M'Uzan, 1983/2013, p. 60). As a result, de M'Uzan asserts that "there is no true boundary between the ego and the non-ego, but a vague transitional zone, a *spectrum of identity* defined by the diverse positions that the narcissistic libido occupies. . . . (1976, pp. 28–29, italics in original).

In Jean Hyppolite's words, ". . . the self never coincides with itself, for it is always other in order to be itself" (1946, p. 150). An identity is created by what is not: a human being can only be human if he or she accepts this fact. While understanding that "I am me . . ." can be acknowledged (in spite of its inherent complications and complexities), to consider which "part of me is not I" is much more difficult to grasp and accept. We are all driven by repressed desires that we will never become aware of, haunted by traumatic experiences of which we know nothing, persecuted by emotional and psychic states of alienation that we cannot comprehend, let alone articulate. The illusion of one day being able to reach another "truer" self, a self that will not suffer from the *extimité* [extimacy] of the self to itself (Lacan, 1953–54), becomes a tragic, as much as a comical, fruitless misunderstanding.

That something can be created through its negativity is a disconcerting idea, but I would suggest that this is what the Freudian uncanny represents in the aesthetic: an encounter with the negative, something secret or repressed in the subject. The negative is represented by the transitory feeling that Freud had at the Acropolis: his "feeling of derealisation", his contention that what he saw was not real. He expanded the description of this feeling thus: ". . . the subject feels that a piece of his own is strange to him . . ." (1936a, pp. 244–245). It belongs to the negative.

There are no certainties about our selves or our pasts; there is no certainty that something has indeed been lost, for it now to be recovered. In its particular mix of familiarity and unfamiliarity, the uncanny is disruptive and unsettling: it is everywhere. In life, in the aesthetic, we face ghosts, doubles, unsolicited apparitions, déjà vu, dangers, anxious anticipations, unsolicited presences brought forward by the negative. All this leads me to conclude that being open—at some level—to experiencing the negative, materialised at times as uncanny, is fundamental to the aesthetic experience. This includes being able to withstand, when faced with the aesthetic object, feelings of depersonalisation (or derealisation), where encountering strangeness and the negative has to be tolerated.

Psychoanalytic and aesthetic concepts share many characteristics, despite their different modes of experience and forms of thought. In both disciplines, the concepts always exceed themselves and cannot be contained within their boundaries. They outclass their definition. In this sense, they are disruptive and unsettling; they inhabit a zone of risk.

As psychoanalysts, we cannot simplify what is extraordinarily multi-layered and exceptionally complex. Therefore, psychoanalysis, as a discipline, can never reach a position where its theory and practice will be able to give a full account of its subject. Not now. Not in the future. The subject of psychoanalysis defies definition, because it is not directly knowable—and yet we need, we want to make sense of it. Psychoanalytic theory, always excessive, cannot be supported by the kind of reductive evidence that would be regarded as "scientific". Evidence cannot be given. Proof cannot be provided. As Carlo Ginzburg argues, it is a form of conjectural knowledge, an indirect, presumptive, intuitive knowledge based on the study of individual cases; it is part of highly qualitative disciplines, which Ginzburg, with undisguised admiration, brings together with the science of the physician and the historian. As argued by him, psychoanalysis is a discipline based on details outside conscious control: ". . . infinitesimal traces permit the comprehension of a deeper, otherwise unattainable reality: traces—more precisely, symptoms (in the case of Freud), clues (in the case of Sherlock Holmes) . . ." (Ginzburg, 1989, p. 101).

Psychoanalysis works through abductive inference, where hypotheses are held awaiting further confirmation—they are put forward as questions. Hence, the analyst's usual form of an interpretation: "I wonder if . . ."; "it sounds as if . . .". It is an attempt at an explanation, never a definite conclusion that can then become a general law.

The term "abduction" was coined by Charles Sanders Peirce in his work on the logic of science. He introduced it to denote a type of non-deductive inference that was different from the already familiar inductive type. In contrast to an inductive inference, abduction is defined as the process of forming explanatory hypotheses. During this process, there might be many hypotheses created and offered for explaining a fact, but only a few would be relatively satisfactory. That an explanation might make meaningful sense would not necessarily imply that there was only one explanation, nor even that it would be the best one. Nevertheless, most importantly, for Peirce abduction is the only logical operation that is capable of introducing new ideas (Peirce, 1903, p. 171; see also Eisele, 1985; Fabbrichesi & Marietti, 2006).

We know from the clinic that certainties arise only from the patient's conviction and by the analyst's conviction. These convictions are fundamental, and yet they are humble: for example, patient and analyst both will re-discover, again and again, that *past* is a misnomer—time passes, but the past persists. We also know, for example, that what we call *working through*, even in its most comprehensive sense, means having to accept that this task will never be fully accomplished. Nothing can be totally changed, completely made good, wholly recovered. Something will remain untouched, undigested, repressed. In other words, the negative will always be present in our lives.

References

Bachelard, G. (1956). Le Cosmos du fer. In: *Derrière le miroir*. Paris: Maeght Éditions, 1964.

Cioran, E. M. (1983). *Ce Maudit moi*. St. Gallen: Édition Erker-Presse.

de M'Uzan, M. (1976). Countertransference and the paradoxical system. *Revue Française de Psychanalyse*, 40 (2): 575–590. Reprinted in: *Death and Identity: Being and the Psycho-Sexual Drama*, ed. M. de M'Uzan, trans. A. Weller. London: Karnac, 2013.

de M'Uzan, M. (1983). The person of myself. *Nouvelle Revue de Psy-*

chanalyse, 28: 193–208. Reprinted in: *Death and Identity: Being and the Psycho-Sexual Drama*, ed. M. de M'Uzan, trans. A. Weller. London: Karnac, 2013.

Eisele, C. (Ed.) (1985). *Historical Perspectives on Peirce's Logic of Science.* New York: Mouton.

Fabbrichesi, R., & Marietti, S. (2006). *Semiotics and Philosophy in Charles Sanders Peirce.* Newcastle: Cambridge Scholars Press.

Freud, S. (1919h). The "uncanny". *Standard Edition, 17*: 217–252.

Freud, S. (1936a). A disturbance of memory on the Acropolis. *Standard Edition, 21*: 237–248.

Ginzburg, C. (1989). *Clues, Myths, and the Historical Method*, trans. J. Tedeschi & A. C. Tedeschi. Baltimore, MD: Johns Hopkins University Press, 2013.

Goldstein, A. M. (2011). "You Have to Make a Choice": A Q&A with Richard Serra on his new sculptures at *Gagosian* [Interview]. *Artinfo (International Edition)*, 28 September.

Green, A. (1997). The intuition of the negative in "Playing and Reality". *International Journal of Psychoanalysis, 78* (6): 1071–1084.

Green, A. (1999). *The Work of the Negative.* London: Free Association Books.

Green, A. (2002). *Time in Psychoanalysis: Some Contradictory Aspects*, trans. A. Weller. London: Free Association Books.

Heidegger, M. (1969). Art and space. *Man and World: An International Philosophical Review, 6* (1): 3–8.

Hillis Miller, J. (1982). *Fiction and Repetition: Seven English Novels.* Oxford: Blackwell.

Hyppolite, J. (1946). *Genesis and Structure in Hegel's Phenomenology*, trans. S. Cherniak & J. Heckman. Evanston, IL: Northwestern University Press, 1974.

Kohon, G. (1999). *No Lost Certainties to Be Recovered.* London: Karnac.

Kohon, G. (2016). *Reflections on the Aesthetic Experience: Psychoanalysis and the Uncanny.* London: Routledge.

Lacan, J. (1953–54). The topic of the imaginary. *The Seminar of Jacques Lacan, Book I: Freud's Papers on Technique*, ed. J.-A. Miller. New York: Norton, 1991.

Paz, O. (1967). Introduction. In: E. Chillida, *Chillida*. Barcelona: Maeght; reprinted Pittsburgh, PA: Pittsburgh International Series, 1980.

Peirce, C. S. (1903). *Collected Papers of Charles Sanders Peirce, Vol. 5*, ed. C. Hatshorne & P. Weiss. Cambridge, MA: Harvard University Press, 1958.

Perelberg, R. J. (2006). The Controversial Discussions and *après-coup*. *International Journal of Psychoanalysis, 87*: 1199–1220.
Perelberg, R. (Ed.) (2007). *Time and Memory*. London: Karnac.
Perelberg, R. (2008). *Time, Space and Phantasy*. London: Routledge.
Rovelli, C. (2014). *Seven Brief Lessons on Physics*, trans. S. Carnell & E. Segre. London: Allen Lane, 2015.
Tóibín, C. (2015). *On Elizabeth Bishop*. Princeton, NJ: Princeton University Press.

CHAPTER FIVE

Intellectual generosity:
the Greekness of Green

Michael Parsons

In this chapter I wish to celebrate Andre Green's intellectual generosity.

Friends and colleagues know how generous he was with his time, his knowledge, and his wisdom. Opponents in debate, though, did not always find him generous. There were some famous occasions when he was uncompromising in his disagreement. The first time I spoke at the Paris Psychoanalytical Society, years ago, André was my discussant. I got a good laugh by saying that while I was naturally very honoured by this, I would wait until after his discussion before thanking him.

The reason André could sometimes be sharp in argument was that he had a clear vision of psychoanalysis whose principles were not to be compromised. That vision was very specific in terms of theory and clinical method, but an important aspect of it was also that psychoanalysis does not live in an ivory tower. It belongs to a larger landscape. The final section of André's book *Key Ideas for a Contemporary Psychoanalysis* (2005) considers how to relate psychoanalysis to other fields of knowledge "at the dawn of the third millennium"; the phrase gives an idea of the scale of his vision. He discusses Aristotle, Kant, and Schopenhauer—and we may remember that the entire second chapter of *The Work of the*

Negative (1999) is about Freud and Hegel. André then surveys the use made of psychoanalysis by Foucault, Ricoeur, Wittgenstein, Derrida, and Habermas, and he treats in similar detail the relation of analytic ideas to neuropsychology and anthropology. He draws on this remarkable breadth of knowledge to illuminate his thinking and makes it available to us as his readers, encouraging us to use it to take our own thinking further. That is what I mean by his intellectual generosity.

This applies especially where literature is concerned, and I want to focus here on André's love affair—one can only call it that—with ancient Greek tragedy and mythology. His book *Un Oeil en trop* [One eye too many] was published in 1969 and translated into English in 1979 as *The Tragic Effect: The Oedipus Complex in Tragedy*. Its first section is called "Orestes and Oedipus: From the Oracle to the Law" and considers primarily the *Oresteia* of Aeschylus. André also wrote a lengthy essay on the myths of Theseus and Oedipus, in a collection of papers called *Psychanalyse et culture Grecque* [Psychoanalysis and Greek culture], which appeared in 1980. Another essay, called "La Magie d'Héphaistos" [The magic of Hephaistos], written in 1971, appeared as the introduction to a book about the myth of Hephaistos by Marie Delcourt, a Belgian classicist. As far as I know, neither of these latter two essays has been translated into English.

It is worth noting how many stage productions of Greek tragedies there have been in recent years. This seems to bear out André's conviction, which I share, that classical Greek literature is an essential part of our culture.

Classicists are sometimes suspicious of psychoanalysts, in case they want to inflict their Freudian preconceptions on a discipline with its own mode of understanding. But André had no interest in imposing analytic theory simplistically on a myth or tragedy. He made a point of respecting the methodology of other disciplines. His chapter on the *Oresteia*, for example, begins with the question: "Who is qualified to write about tragedy?"

> We have the Hellenist or the philologist, concerned with literal accuracy, mistrustful of any interpretation that sacrifices accuracy in an attempt to re-establish a full meaning, which even today remains obscure: we have the tragic actor, concerned in his interpretation to convey the tragic emotion to his audience. [1979, p. 35]

And in the essay on Hephaistos, he writes of "the patient work of enumeration, classification, dating and the attribution of origins" (1971, p. vii) that the scholar of mythology must undertake. Alongside this recognition, however, he makes a similar claim for psychoanalysis. The passage from the *Oresteia* chapter continues:

> Is there, between these two [the Hellenist and the tragic actor] a place for a psychoanalytic commentator, sharing with the other two the common ground of hermeneutics . . . ? The psychoanalyst would strive, then, to rediscover that letter and that flesh of tragedy reunited with his own truth. [1979, p. 35]

In the Hephaistos essay, the acknowledgment of the scholar's "patient work" is followed by the claim that a myth is "a construction like the secondary elaboration of a dream". This, says André, sends the scholar, with his academic commentaries, back to the drawing board and highlights instead the traces left in the story by those reference points around which the analyst's work is organised; these André defines as "desire and its relation to sexuality and aggressiveness" (1971, p. viii). Again, near the beginning of the essay on Oedipus and Theseus, André says explicitly that the subjectivity that informs the analyst's approach can illuminate details that escape the scholar of classical literature or mythology (1980, p. 110).

There seems to be a certain conflict here. André has a genuine respect for classical scholarship, and sometimes he is clearly looking for a two-way traffic between it and psychoanalysis. At other times he reveals a conviction that those who regard literature and mythology as their own proper territory are in some way restricted, while he, as a psychoanalyst, has a unique contribution to offer that is beyond their reach. How he defines psychoanalysis is part of that, and the definition I have just quoted—that it deals with the relation of desire to aggression and sexuality—is worth noting. I think the conflict between these two attitudes reflects a tension that pervades André's work more generally, one that I shall come back to.

There is no space here to go into all that André has to say about the *Oresteia*, Oedipus, Theseus, and Hephaistos. One thing these essays reveal consistently, though, is that the myths are more mobile and fluid than we might expect. It is no surprise for

Oedipus to appear in the title of the two most substantial pieces: the chapter "Orestes and Oedipus" in *The Tragic Effect* (1979) and the essay "Thésée et Oedipe [Theseus and Oedipus]" (1980). The story of Oedipus is the foundation myth of psychoanalysis. This sounds rather fixed and static, as though the myth is what it is, we know what the story consists of, and then Freud comes along and reveals its implications: job done. I suspect Freud did think something like that, and, indeed, André suggests reasons why this is, as he puts it, "the reference myth for psychoanalysts" (1980, p. 155): it deals with the essential nature of kinship and defines a person in terms of his relation to his parents; it shows that the search for truth is inescapably linked to the search for origins; crucial elements in the unfolding of the narrative function both as obstacles to knowledge and sources of knowledge (as Sophocles dramatised so clearly); and Oedipus solves the riddle of the Sphinx ("What goes on four legs in the morning, two legs at midday, and three legs in the evening?") by realising that the subject of the riddle is mankind itself. At the same time, however, André remarks that no myth, considered on its own, can represent every aspect of the Oedipus complex. The negative Oedipus complex, for example, involving the boy's passive love for the father and hostility towards the mother, has no place in the story of Oedipus; neither does the shift from a boy's rivalry with his father to identification with him, which is such a crucially important part of oedipal development.

In this sense, André finds the myth of Oedipus incomplete. He goes on to show that aspects of oedipal development that are missing from the story of Oedipus turn up in the story of Theseus. There are strong links between the two myths, which André comes at by way of an unexpected literary reference. André Gide's novel *Theseus* (1946) imagines the hero telling his life story, and André (Green, that is) quotes a passage where Theseus remembers his encounter at Colonus with the blind, exiled Oedipus. Theseus calls this the "supreme confrontation at the crossroads of our two careers" and regards it as his personal "crowning glory" (Green, 1980, p. 110). Offering the reader such an interesting link between Sophocles and twentieth-century literature is another example of André's intellectual generosity. He notes the crucial connection between the two figures that Gide has spotlighted. Theseus was illegitimately fathered by Aegeus, king of Athens, in Troizen, where he was brought up by his mother Aethra. Aegeus left behind in Troizen tokens—a sword and sandals—for Theseus to discover, if he were ever strong enough to lift the rock that concealed them. When Theseus found these and realised his true identity, he travelled to Athens and presented himself to Aegeus. Both Oedipus and Theseus, therefore, were boys abandoned by their fathers and brought up in a foreign city. Both learnt that they were not who they thought they were—Theseus at the beginning of his story, Oedipus too late, at the end of his. Both went journeying, killing monsters on the way—Theseus from Troizen to Athens, putting various brigands and murderers to death as he went, Oedipus killing the Sphinx in his flight from Corinth to Thebes. And both finally encountered, for better or worse, their true fathers.

Theseus was also responsible for the death of his father Aegeus—not with his own hand, like Oedipus, but by an indirect parricide. The ship that took Theseus to Crete as a prospective victim for the Minotaur was supposed, on its return, to wear black sails if he were dead, but white if he were still alive. Theseus forgot about this, and his father, seeing the ship with black sails, killed himself by leaping from a cliff.

Having established the "reverberation", as he puts it (1980, p. 157), between the two myths, André picks up on important differences. When Theseus determines to go to Athens, Aethra pleads with him not to leave her, but he refuses to stay and sets out on the journey to his father. André remarks that this shows the negative Oedipus complex—the boy's rejection of his mother and desire to be close to his father—that is missing from the story of Oedipus. The outcome of the two parricides is also very different. In Oedipus' case it is catastrophic: he blinds himself, loses his throne, and becomes a polluted exile. Theseus, however, on learning he is responsible for his father's death, takes over the throne and reigns in his father's place. Here is the successful outcome of the Oedipus complex, by the son's identification with the father: the second element of oedipal development that is absent in the myth of Oedipus.

For André, the myth of Theseus thus rounds out and completes the myth of Oedipus. The same freedom of observation and interpretation appears in his treatment of the myths of Hephaistos and Prometheus. Briefly, André's argument runs as follows. Hephaistos was the son of Hera by parthenogenesis, and he wielded the axe that split the skull of Zeus so that Athena could be born: two acts of exceptional generation. He was also a smith, the god of fire and craftsmanship. These generative and creative qualities are displaced into the myth of Prometheus, where they are further developed. Prometheus stole the gift of fire from the gods—primarily from Hephaistos, the god whose forge was always aflame. For this, he was chained to a rock where every day an eagle was sent by Zeus to eviscerate him and shred his liver. Prometheus gave fire to mankind, and he is also said, through his punishment, to have given man the gift of divination by examining the entrails of sacrificial animals. The gift of fire made available to humanity the skills of Hephaistos: metallurgy and craftsmanship, leading to agriculture and eventually all that we would now consider under the heading of science. The gift of divination denotes the capacity to imagine the future and put the first gift to work in the service of humanity. What strikes me here is the intellectual freedom that makes it possible for André to see one myth so fruitfully as the evolution of another, not obviously related one.

This capacity to make creative connections also shows itself when André comes to consider Greek tragedy: the *Oresteia* in particular. He looks beyond Aeschylus, in two directions. Without going into detail, I would like to give some idea of André's range and ingenuity in this area. First he compares Orestes, and the story of the house of Atreus, with the legends surrounding Oedipus. He draws fascinating parallels and contrasts.

> Oedipus commits parricide and incest, Orestes commits matricide and champions the cause of his father. In the *Oresteia* the mother does not commit incest, but is the agent of the parricide. In short, both situations focus on the study of triangular relationships, of the subject's relation to his progenitors. . . . Studying this comparison reveals an opposition so deep that it is more properly to be considered as a "complementarity". [1979, p. 38]

What does André mean by this? In the House of Atreus Agamemnon, Clytemnestra, and (ambiguously) Orestes provoke the gods and bring their catastrophic fates on themselves. Violence and vengeance are the conscious motivations of the central characters in the trilogy. Oedipus' parents, on the other hand, and Oedipus himself, in leaving Corinth and the couple he believes to be his parents, do all they can to prevent Apollo's oracle from being fulfilled. The central characters in this story are trying to avoid damaging the family; the tragedy unfolds not because of their destructiveness, as in the *Oresteia*, but despite their efforts not to be destructive. The tragedy of Oedipus, says André, is centrifugal. Attempts to avert disaster involve exile, flight, and distance: Oedipus' parents put their baby out on the mountain, Oedipus mistakenly flees from Corinth to Thebes, he sends to Delphi for a solution to the plague. The *Oresteia*, by contrast, is centripetal. There is no attempt to avert disaster: its inevitability is taken for granted, as everything intensifies at the centre. Agamemnon returns home from war to be murdered by Clytemnestra; Orestes returns home from exile to find Electra consumed with desire for vengeance; and the two of them murder Clytemnestra in the very spot where she killed their father.

Having outlined this "complementary opposition" between the two legends, André comments as follows:

> These two images suggest two types of movement in the unconscious. In the first, the repressed undergoes constant displacements that remove the expression of its content ever further away in its distortions and disguises. In the second, on the other hand, the unconscious is presented with unusual transparency, as the bearer of an excess of signification; so what is ordinarily veiled or minimised is expressed with a crudity that suggests some defect in its symbolisation. [1979, p. 39]

I find that extremely interesting psychoanalytically, and respectful at the same time of the literary qualities of the work.

The same thing applies to the second direction in which André looks beyond Aeschylus. The *Oresteia* contains the only instance where we have surviving plays by all three of the great Greek tragedians on the same subject. Orestes' return and Clytemnestra's murder by him and Electra occur in the second play of the trilogy, *Choephoroi*, and Sophocles and Euripides each wrote an *Electra*, dealing with the same events. An important element of the traditional story is a dream that Clytemnestra has on the night before

Orestes reveals himself. André again shows the openness of his approach, as well as his sheer enjoyment of Greek tragedy, as he discusses how differently the three dramatists treat this dream.

In *Choephoroi*, Clytemnestra dreams that she gives birth to a snake, which she swaddles and puts to her breast. It bites the nipple and brings forth both milk and blood. In Sophocles' *Electra*, she dreams that Agamemnon comes back to life, holding his royal sceptre. He plants it by the altar of the house, where it sprouts into a tree whose shadow covers all Mycaenae. In the *Electra* of Euripides, the dream is omitted; there is no reference to it.

The dream of the snake in *Choephoroi* has a constricted, oppressive physicality, with the snake moving from Clytemnestra's womb to her breast and destroying both. André contrasts this with the open space outside the palace and the expansiveness of the branching tree, in the dream in Sophocles' *Electra*.

The symbolism in *Choephoroi* embraces Orestes as the snake to which Clytemnestra gave birth; the snake as his phallic potency directed towards his mother, and his erotic desire for her breast, fused with his desire to destroy her; and Clytemnestra's erotic desire for her son, fused again with her destructiveness, her breast being full of blood as well as milk. The chthonic, underground nature of the snake in classical Greek symbolism lets it also represent Agamemnon returning from the world of the dead. Into this single terrifying image Aeschylus compresses all the horror of what is happening in the moment.

André notes how in Sophocles' *Electra*, the symbolism is much less dense, and instead of loading the instant with horror, as Aeschylus does, it directs attention away from the present. Agamemnon reappears from the past, undisguised, with the sceptre he carried when he used to be king. The tree, spreading its branches over Mycenae, points towards the future and the growth of new possibilities. The phallic symbolism of the sceptre is the same as the phallic symbolism of the snake, and the identification of Orestes with his father, as his arrival brings doom to Clytemnestra, is still there. However, where the *Oresteia* is a continuous nightmare that is relieved only at the end of the trilogy, Sophocles is writing a different sort of play, about light rather than darkness, and he does not need the overload of horror that Aeschylus required.

When it comes to Euripides—no dream at all! What has happened to it? Euripides' play is centred, much more than the other two, on Electra. In André's view, although the oedipal framework is still present, this is basically a play about femininity. Electra has been married off to a peasant. Clytemnestra is keeping herself safe inside the palace, well aware that if Orestes returns, her life is in danger. Electra tricks her into coming out by pretending to be having a baby; the ceremony of naming the child will require the presence of Clytemnestra. Any child of Electra's must represent a threat to Clytemnestra, and André's interpretation is that with this make-believe pregnancy, Electra is expressing her fantasy of giving birth herself to a child who will kill Clytemnestra in revenge for Agamemnon's death. It would be a child of Agamemnon's, of course, who would want to avenge him. Electra's unconscious fantasy, therefore, is of having a child by her father, and this fantasy child who will avenge Agamemnon is none other than Orestes. By sending word that she is having a baby, Electra unconsciously communicates to Clytemnestra that a child of Agamemnon's, to whom Clytemnestra gave birth, who escaped into exile, is now being re–produced by Electra. Clytemnestra's desire, conscious or unconscious, to murder this child, will draw her out of the palace to be murdered herself. I am slightly elaborating what André says, but what I understand him to mean is that Electra's invention unconsciously conveys both her own oedipal desire, the linked erotic and matricidal desire of Orestes, and the linked erotic and murderous desire of Clytemnestra towards Orestes. With all this unconsciously present already, the twist that Euripides has given to the story renders the dream redundant: there is no need for it.

I hope I have conveyed the play of André's mind as he brought psychoanalytic ideas to bear on Greek mythology and tragedy. Could one say that he made this approach work in the way he did by cherry-picking myths and plays that were susceptible to such an approach? This would be an ungenerous accusation. André was making use of the mythology and literature that have animated our culture to animate further our contemporary and future culture. What one might, perhaps, want to pick up on is a tension between a certain purism in André's view of psychoanalysis, and the flexibility and openness to the unexpected that show through in his work that I have been describing. This tension may have shown itself sometimes in discussions, when one could see André slipping into a rather dogmatic stance and then having to recover himself from that. He wrote *The Tragic Effect* in the 1960s, at the height of his engagement with Lacan's ideas and his mantra of a return to Freud. As I indicated, I think Freud did get a bit stuck in a somewhat monolithic view of the Oedipus legend—a stuckness of which André, as I have shown, was wonderfully free. But you will also recall André's statement, which I quoted earlier: that the essential concern of psychoanalysis is with desire and its relation to sexuality and aggressiveness. That seems to me, in its pared-down austerity, not incorrect but a somewhat narrow definition of psychoanalysis, which belongs, perhaps, to its time. The essay on Hephaistos in which it appears was published in 1971, with André battling by then to sort out his relationship with Lacan. What a remarkable distance André travelled in the thirty years between that and the rich complexity of *Key Ideas for a Contemporary Psychoanalysis* (2005)—a book that still demonstrates, nonetheless, the rigour of his thinking about psychoanalysis. His struggle to reconcile a strict insistence on preserving the specificity of psychoanalysis, with the creativity of his mind that kept bursting out in one direction after another, was exemplary.

References

Gide, A. (1946). *Theseus*, trans. A. Brown. London: Hesperus, 2002.

Green, A. (1971). La Magie d'Héphaistos. In: M. Delcourt, *Héphaistos ou la légende du magicien* (pp. vii–xxiii). Paris: Les Belles Lettres, 1982.

Green, A. (1979). *The Tragic Effect: The Oedipus Complex in Tragedy*. Cambridge: Cambridge University Press. [First published as: *Un Oeil en trop*. Paris: Les Editions de Minuit, 1969.]

Green, A. (1980). Thésée et Oedipe. In: *Psychanalyse et culture Grecque* (pp. 109–158). Paris: Les Belles Lettres.

Green, A. (1999). *The Work of the Negative*. London: Free Association Books.

Green, A. (2005). *Key Ideas for a Contemporary Psychoanalysis: Misrecognition and Recognition of the Unconscious*, trans. A. Weller. London: Routledge.

CHAPTER SIX

An interview with André Green: on a psychoanalytic journey from 1960 to 2011

Fernando Urribarri

U*rribarri:* To begin with let us address your intellectual journey . . .

Green: It could be explained by giving geographical, historic, and—undoubtedly—cultural reasons. I started by having a psychiatric training. But from the very beginning of our training we were aware in France that things were thought of in an original way, in a different way from the thinking in England, the USA, or South America.

After undergoing my training in French psychiatry, I needed to make a decision about a situation that troubled me regarding the first split of the SPP [Société Psychanalytique de Paris], in 1953, which had led to the departure from the SPP of those who left it to found another analytic movement, essentially around Lagache and Lacan. Right at the time that I began my analytic training, I was faced with the dilemma of where I should go. Lacan was already quite notorious. And he lured with him a number of personalities who were to play an important role in the future of psychoanalysis in France, although later they were to leave Lacan. Among them, the closest to me was my dear friend Rosolato. From working at St. Anne's [Hospital]

I knew Laplanche, and—more distantly—I got to know Pontalis, Piera Aulagnier, Anzieu, all these authors—a generation that was my generation, people with whom friendship ties were above institutional differences. Finally I decided to apply at the SPP because already by then I did not like certain attitudes of Lacan. Lacan treated his disciples unkindly, and I did not want to be mistreated by him. The great event at that time was the Bonneval Colloquy. It was the first encounter between the SPP people and Lacan and his disciples.

Urribarri: You are referring to the year 1960, about "The Unconscious"—am I right?

Green: Yes. As I have often said, that Colloquy was a "Trafalgar" for the SPP people, who, in the debates, were unable to stand up against the arguments of Lacan's disciples and Lacan himself. So I wrote an article, published in *Les Temps Modernes* [1962], that you know well.

Urribarri: The article on the Freudian unconscious and contemporary French psychoanalysis.

Green: Exactly. And then, early on, I expressed my objections regarding Lacan. In reading Lacan, one could see that he did not take into account what Freud said about affect—the distinction drawn by Freud between representation and affect. For Lacan, affect has no interest; it is not mentioned, it is not an issue—neither psychoanalytic nor scientific—for him. And it is from this experience that I decided to write *The Fabric of Affect and Psychoanalytic Discourse* [French edition, 1973/English translation, 1999]. When Lacan had the book in his hands, he was furious. He even renamed the book, by a play on his own words, and called it "The abject". But I understood him. I took the decision to criticise him. If he did not like it, too bad.

Before this episode he had tried to lure me into his group. I had started to frequent his seminar after Bonneval and he started to court me. He used to say to me that I should be part of his group, that my place was beside him. And even if I was fascinated by him, his talent, his personality, his culture. . . . I followed him from 1960 until 1967 and then I took distance . . .

Urribarri: When you say that he "he tried to lure" you, it seems to me that you are referring to a time after the Bonneval meeting . . .

Green: Yes. After Bonneval I attended his seminar, and he started courting me insistently, "That I must become part of his group, that my place was by his side". I was fascinated by this man, by his talent, his personality and culture. And if I deserve any credit, it is the fact that I refused to be seduced by him, in spite of his great seductive power. So, I followed him from 1960 to 1967 and then I created a distance from him.

What people usually do not know is that in 1961—that is, a year after Bonneval—it was the IPA Congress in London, and with some young colleagues we went to London and got in touch with English analysts. And that contact was a true revelation to me. I had the chance of personally meeting analysts such as John Klauber, Herbert Rosenfeld, and even Winnicott. And I was so impressed that I told myself, what we do in France is not psychoanalysis; it is *discourse,* denuded of clinical thought. British clinical thought was nourished by a post-Freudian conceptualisation of great force.

So from 1960 on I had Lacan on one side, and the English analysts on the other. And then, at Pontalis's *Nouvelle Revue de Psychanalyse* (NRP), Masud Khan became part of the Pontalis staff and helped us know Winnicott better. At that time, around the NRP group, a new current in France had arisen, showing a strong interest in Winnicott and allowing us to stray a little from the Lacanian influence.

Urribarri: Are those to whom you often refer as the *Post-Lacanians?*

Green: Those who were *going to become Post-Lacanians*—to the extent, we should not forget, that there was a new split that separated them from Lacan—Laplanche, Pontalis, Anzieu, and shortly thereafter Aulagnier. And they would not refer in the same way to Lacan, with the same dogmatism, as those who decided to remain with Lacan. For me this explains many things. Because Lacan, after two splits, fell completely out of friendship with them—that is, the disciples that he was counting on had made another choice, and he became an enemy of his own disciples. For example, at Bonneval there were Laplanche and Leclaire . . .

Urribarri: Laplanche and Leclaire who represented Lacan . . .

Green: Yes, and then Lacan was going to turn violently against Laplanche.

Urribarri: Really, how so?

Green: By saying that Laplanche does not understand anything he says, that he means something else. And it is true that there are some slight differences. In the middle of this, I found myself listening. And for the most part I felt close to the Post-Lacanians, and I became good friends with them. From a certain moment, probably after 1967, before *The Fabric of Affect and Psychoanalytic Discourse* [1973/1999], I started to follow an independent path, telling myself that there were certain things people were not talking about.

Urribarri: Among those things was the question of narcissism in relation to the death drive?

Green: Not yet about the death drive, but to narcissism, yes. The problem was that before Lacan the only consistent thinking at the SPP was that of Bouvet, with his development of object relations. Bouvet had developed his vision, but he had not taken narcissism enough into account. And the question of narcissism already interested me. Plus, there was a second subject: the borderline cases, whose existence had been pointed out to me by the English. So it was because of these that I started working. I started with the writing of the London Report, in 1975, dedicated to Winnicott, who had just passed away. And after the Report came narcissism—my conception of narcissism, which was neither that of Grunberger, nor that of Lacan. I introduced, on my part, the double conception of a positive narcissism and a negative narcissism. From then on, Lacan understood that I had left Lacanian thinking. Certainly I was interested, but I was not a militant as he wished all of us to become. So, the first part of the journey: affect, living speech, non-neurotic structures, and narcissism.

Urribarri: Before continuing, could you tell me the main contributions of your book on affect?

Green: I would rather talk about my ideas about affect than about my book. They play an important role, because it is quite obvious that Lacan made a mistake by disregarding it. For the reasons that I have already mentioned, affect is placed outside the scientific quest of language, so he does not talk about "that". But the analysts saw that psychoanalytic theory cannot minimise the role of affect. That is why I wrote *The Fabric of Affect and Psychoanalytic Discourse* in 1973. But some years later I wrote about affect for the 1999 Chile Congress, and after my report for the Congress, the American analysts openly said that they did not understand anything at all, that they did not know what to do with it.

Urribarri: You are referring to the 1999 article that is in your book *La Pensée clinique* [2002], right?

Green: Yes, this article also gives a new meaning to *The Fabric of Affect and Psychoanalytic Discourse*. I consider my Santiago report an important text for me; the people who had to discuss it had never actually read it, because it was deemed too complex.

Urribarri: So as to follow the historic thread, in *The Fabric of Affect and Psychoanalytic Discourse* you introduced the notion of "heterogeneity of the signifier". Would you care to elaborate on this idea?

Green: Yes, it is easy. There are two options. It is based on whether or not one has the Freudian reference in mind. If one speaks outside the Freudian reference, one can say anything. But if one follows Freud's perspective, the heterogeneity of the signifier becomes apparent. It is not about the Saussurean signifier, but the Lacanian signifier. If we see the references within which Freudian theory is constructed, the signifier cannot be reduced to word-representation. It is divided into different parts of the theoretical arsenal: thing-representation, word-representation, affect, corporal states, acts, and so forth. These are the instruments through which an analyst thinks. It is an array. And this array is the contrary of the linguistic signifier—because we consider that all of these elements, such as representations of things, of words, of bodily states, become a panoply of different elements of analytic communication, and that is why I speak about heterogeneity. Because I think it is quite important. Language, by definition, is the result of homogenisation. This very same homogenisation is . . . language! In linguistics, that is why one cannot speak about anything but language. If one tries to do so, one runs into many difficulties.

Urribarri: I would like to move forward. After your work on affect came a book that became a classic on narcissism: *Life Narcissism, Death Narcissism* [1983/2001]. I would like to know your personal conception of narcissism . . .

Green: I do not wish to go backwards, but my own conception of narcissism derives from the following question: "What becomes of narcissism after the second drive theory?" As you know, many people make a superficial reading of it and maintain that Freud is no longer interested in narcissism. The theory based on object libido and narcissistic libido is replaced with the pair made of life drive and death drive The fact that the second drive theory eclipses narcissism brings up the question of what became of narcissism. I tell myself that if the narcissistic theory is followed by the second drive theory, it is possible to find already there an implicit theory that includes life drive and death drive. Therefore, one can say that from the death drive derives negative narcissism, from the life drive derives positive narcissism. Negative narcissism is my invention. And there are a certain number of authors who find this concept useful to understand certain things—but not about the same patients, but about other patients who were not approached by theory . . .

Urribarri: Do you mean "by classic theory"?

Green: Yes. Let us take, for example, anorexia.

Urribarri: In your book [*Life Narcissism*] you give an example that has become paradigmatic, and it is the *dead mother* complex.

Green: Yes, one can say that, exactly. It is an original contribution. It tries to account for some part of the pathology that, at the time, had not been the subject of a coherent theorisation. Like anorexia, or what Freud refers to—but did not develop—in three pages of a chapter in *Inhibition, Symptoms and Anxiety* on inhibition [1926d (1925)]. I think Freud says that inhibition cannot be explained by the theory of the neuroses. We are in the realm of narcissism. Besides, my work stems from a different source: the non-neurotic structures.

Urribarri: Before talking about this fundamental chapter, I would like to ask you a question about the book on narcissism, because I have the impression that already there you introduced a major concept—although it had appeared in some of your previous writings as well. It constitutes a very personal conceptual synthesis: I am referring to the notion of *framing structure*.

Green: Oh, yes, the *framing structure* notion comes from a finding in my own theoretical research. I began by considering the brief footnote by Freud about negative hallucination [1917d (1915), p. 232n.]. I felt quite impressed. I said to myself: he is saying something essential, but how come he does not make any further references later on? Freud says that if there is any interest in hallucination, one should not start from the positive hallucination but from studying negative hallucination. Negative hallucination exists in Freud works, but only at the beginning of his thinking, and then he abandons the subject. I considered that there was something to understand, to use, to draw from negative hallucination. What you bring back with your remark is the role I give it within the framing structure. There I say that there is a negative hallucination of the mother that remains there beyond her representation. Why is this a *framing structure*? Because I considered that the infant who is held by its mother later introjects the framing given by the body of the mother, the way she holds him or her, and so on, and it is after this negative moment that representations can occupy the empty space created by the negative hallucination. The *framing structure* is important . . .

Urribarri: Would you say that the *framing structure* frames the ego? Or does it frame narcissism?

Green: Maybe narcissism . . . but I would not wish to link it to a psychic instance. In particular, I consider it as a structure that gives framing . . .

Urribarri: . . . that serves to create or establish the distinction between inside and outside?

Green: Yes, it is thanks to that that the ["positive"] representations may find or have a place. That is the *framing structure.* It is in *Life Narcissism, Death Narcissism,* in 1983. And I still value that, and some of my contemporary colleagues use it. But already then, there is a notion that analysts do not like so much: that of the negative. They pose the question: what is the negative? Is it negative transference? Is it the negative therapeutic reaction? This seems to me a very restrictive interpretation of the richness of the concept of the negative, which is vaster, which allows us to reflect not only on the negative aspects but on what *constitutes*—like a negative in photography—a necessary stage for the becoming of the positive, of the representation. That is the way of introducing the negative that I maintain culminates in *The Work of the Negative* [1995/1999], which is probably the most important work I have written.

Urribarri: Oh, really . . . ?

Green: I think so, yes . . .

Urribarri: Before writing the book, you had previously explored another subject that implies the notion of the negative—combined, complicated, and complexed—with that of the positive. Because the notion of the negative traverses the book after the one on narcissism [1983]. It was published in all languages spoken in the psychoanalytic world, and it is titled *On Private Madness* [1986].

Green: *On Private Madness* belongs to my beginnings . . .

Urribarri: I understand that for you—as an author—it represents something from the past.

Green: But, nevertheless, I love *On Private Madness* . . .

Urribarri: Great! Let us talk about that love! Why do you talk about "private madness"?

Green: Why "private madness"? Well, because it is a way of introducing the hypothesis that certain transferences are felt by the patient as the only place, the only site, where he or she feels able to speak about what is his or her madness. I say it is private because outside that situation we would not say he or she is psychotic. We do not have any sign of a mental functioning dictated by psychosis, and here we shall make a distinction that is in an article that you are very familiar with, "Passions and Their Vicissitudes" [1980]—the distinction between madness and psychosis. It is said that everyone is mad; but the psychotics are also ill.

Urribarri: It is remarkable that you give a great deal of importance to life narcissism and death narcissism, but your approach is different from what was said before or even today. You propose to relate narcissist "failures" with the drive aspect. That is to say, instead of opposing—in a classic way—narcissism with the object, you speak of passion. You put in a dialectic relationship a passionate drive movement and a narcissistic attachment to the object. Am I correct?

Green: Yes, yes, it is true, because the essence of narcissism cannot be reduced to the narcissistic character. In my opinion, what constitutes the power in narcissism is that it is about a relation from which there is no way out—one that prevents the person from opening to other objects that offer a way out.

Urribarri: In the beginning of the 1990s you published *The Work of the Negative*. Could you tell us why you felt the urge to write a book dedicated to this concept?

Green: It is not easy to tell that in a few words. The notion of "the work of the negative" I took from an expression by Hegel. But contrary to what some people may think, Hegel does not say much about it. It cannot be said that I based my text on Hegel's work and ideas. What initially interested me was the idea of the negative, the work of the negative, which plays a fundamental role in analysis. Because I consider, with absolute conviction, that a fundamental element in analytic thought is played by drive. Drive that manifests itself by being a force in excess. If we wish to stay alive, if we wish to continue being part of the community of civilised beings, we must neutralise that excessive force of the drives. This is at the foundation of the theory of repression. But it is also at the very bottom of certain perils that are postulated by psychoanalysis, such as acting out—the impossibility of containing, that which goes over the individual's capacity for internal elaboration and forces him to act out. On the other hand, this will open another line of thought about the negative, which corresponds to the negative considered in its excessive dimension but also in the rejection of any attempt to inhibit an impulse—for instance, to act out. You know that the range of the negative covers a panoply of problems that cannot be abridged. One must try to see the different sectors in which the negative expresses itself. One of the aspects of the negative is linked to the issue of the expression of destructiveness.

Urribarri: So as to be accurate, without simplifying it, it could be said that your theory distinguishes two dimensions of the work of the negative, the first of which is fundamental for structuring the psyche to become a member of the civilised community. It is the example of repression: primary repression structures the psyche. But in a dialectic and complex relation, there is another dimension of the negative that can become de-structuring and even destructive. Is this appreciation correct?

Green: Totally correct.

Urribarri: You were going to say something about the destructive aspect . . .

Green: At a certain point in my journey, I realised that there cannot be a serious psychoanalytic theory without following Freud in the last stages of his thinking—that is to say, the second drive theory. I do not consider that the death drive is something one "does or does not believe", as Freud said at the beginning, but that it represents an element of a Freudian logic that is extremely powerful. Therefore, psychoanalysis evolves through taking on destructiveness in the form of the work of the negative. We see all the richness of the negative, that on a first definition is necessary to the construction of the psyche battling against the more raw aspects. Freud starts with perversion, which has to do with that rawness. And on the other side there is a negative that today I call "radical negative", that only says "NO!"—that does not look for either commitment or sublimation. This allows us to imagine this radical negativity as something essential that does not have to do with the structuring negative: it just says "No". It is not the converse of yes. It is "no" without any reference to the positive. Let's say, for the sake of illustration, that this could resemble a certain form of obstinacy: "NO is NO!"—says the patient—"you will not make me admit with your interpretations that there is something positive behind the negative. No is no!"

Urribarri: Is it about a movement of the death drive, or is about a fixation on hate? Or is it both working together?

Green: Yes, it is about both.

Urribarri: One last question: in the first chapters of *On Private Madness* you refer to the borderline cases and propose four mechanisms of defence that are basic or typical: expulsion via action, somatic exclusion, splitting, and primary depression. This last concept is then replaced by another more accurate one: decathexis.

Green: These ideas that you are referring to were in the London Report [1975]. As time went by, I no longer believed in that set-up. I realised that I was not going deep enough, to the bottom of the matter. Some ideas are still worth it, of course, such as the replacement of repression by splitting, or what you have just pointed out, such as the decathexis mechanism. These are interesting observations. But recently I wrote an article called "Les cas limite" ["Borderline cases: From private madness to the destructive and death drives", 2011a]. The further I go, the more I understand that these manifestations of borderline cases are determined by a coefficient of destruction that is unable to be worked through. So I dedicated myself to deepening the study of Freudian theory, regarding the destructive drive, in a book I wrote and which I continue considering a good book.

Urribarri: Do you refer to *Pourquoi les pulsions de destruction ou de mort*? [Why the destructive or death drives?] [Green, 2007]?

Green: Yes. There I state the following: that after Freud, no one wants to listen to anyone talking about the death drive, but everything that is put there to replace it to have a clearer conception sends us back to the death drive. Winnicott says he does not accept the death drive, but when we read him carefully, he says: "death drive no, but destructiveness yes". But where does destructiveness come from? We see him entangling himself to explain it. A similar situation with other authors: Pierre Marty [1976] does not want to deal with the death drive, and he speaks of individual movements . . .

Urribarri: . . . of disorganisation.

Green: Yes. But in the end it is another version that Marty proposes about what was said by Freud about the death drive. I say that currently there is a problem about the death drive, due to the rejection by authors of the way Freud described it. And there are some attempts of reformulations to overcome the formulation presented by Freud. Very well. But that does not change the problem: the problem is that there is destructiveness, admitted by these authors, that hinders analytic work.

Urribarri: Could you comment about your own vision of destructiveness? Does it present a double orientation, internal and external?

Green: As you have pointed out, I think I have tried to take into account clinical practice based on my own experience. I do not think I agree with Freud's view about the original position of the death drive. I am not convinced that we are born with an amount of death drive that is going to evolve. I say that circumstances as we go through life will favour a surge of the death drive, or will moderate it. In other words, I agree on considering the death drive in relation to the life drive. I try to make the theory more in tune with clinical practice. You see, there is, in that book of mine, an important passage, in which I take a description by Freud, saying that narcissism plays a fundamental role, which I consider quite fair . . .

Urribarri: You are referring to a passage that is in *Beyond the Pleasure Principle* [1920g]. How does he make it work?

Green: Contrary to a frequent, banal position that says: "How can death drive exist before life drive?" expressed by those who follow a common-sense line of reasoning. But that does not represent the way Freud was thinking. Freud thought that the first drive is the death drive. Why? Because it agrees with his idea that the death drive aspires to go backwards, that it opposes progress. If he says that the death drive comes first, it is because it opposes progress. In my opinion that first progress should be called cathexis, but it is not a drive. The death drive does not feature yet: later it will try to disorganise life acquisitions. And Freud asks what it is that opposes the first action of death drive: it is narcissism.[1] It is a noteworthy idea, it is very strong! Why? If one thinks about psychosomatics, one realises that there is some truth to it in Freud. In psychosomatics, internal destructiveness against the body develops from a failure of narcissism. These are people who are not able to defend themselves by making narcissism reject destructiveness, and so they fall into psychosomatic destructiveness. So the idea that narcissism is the first resistance against destruction seems interesting to me.

Urribarri: This recent finding of the passage in Freud implies a remarkable convergence with the central role played by the object that you have been pointing out for a number of years.

Green: Yes, yes! But it is not me who says so, it is Freud!

Urribarri: I realise that . . .

Green: Freud tries a developmental outline and manages to say things that no one "makes him say". He approaches the manifestations of destructiveness and says that it is at the level of object libido that we see the death drive operate. It is the object that is important. It is the love object that is important. You understand that these are notes taken by Freud that are essential to clinical practice. When you have to deal with a borderline or similar patient, you have to deal with the lacks and failures of the love of the object.

Urribarri: Speaking of which, I would like to ask you if you still consider important some conceptualisations you propose in order to rethink these issues in terms of objectalising and de-objectalising functions. Does the de-objectalising function correspond to what you just described?

Green: It corresponds to the destruction drive. The main feature of the de-objectalising function is decathexis. Decathexis prevents cathexis and also prevents the display of life drives.

Urribarri: I would like to underline how interesting and clinically suggestive this thesis turns out to be. Even if your formulation is abstract, it connects to our "clinical thought", when you say that we should think of death drive not only in relation to what has just been mentioned, but also with the perspective of a dialogue that does not go well between drive and object.

Green. Yes, because the object, among its basic functions, is in charge of the intricacy.

Urribarri: The cathexis. You speak of the primary object . . .

Green: The primary object helps the fusion process. If the object does not play its role or if it is a failed object functioning or an unavailable object drive, defusion takes the lead, and when this happens, the death drive frees itself.

Urribarri: Following your thinking and following the internal coherence of your journey, conceptually we come across some of your ideas that you put in writing in the mid-1990s. In these works you systematically propose an articulation between the intrapsychic and the inter-subjective by formulating the pair "drive–object".

Green: Having this in mind, I can go back to the question you asked me before—the one I did not answer. Neuroses are characterised by an intrapsychic disorder. That is to say, the question about the object in neuroses does not have too much weight. Neurosis is a construction of the subject. It is internal, intra-pyschic. If we have to take the inter-subjective aspect into account, it is because the object brings its difficulties to the solution of problems.

Urribarri: For example?

Green: Everything written by Winnicott. He says that the environment is not sufficiently taken into account. People often speak gibberish when they consider Winnicott to be an "environmentalist". What he says is that it is not the same to have a psychotic mother as to have a "good-enough mother". And you are right. They are not the same pathology. If you are dealing with a pathology that implies a psychotic mother, you must consider the inter-subjective dimension and not only the intrapsychic one, because the patient has to fight against his or her own impulses while having to fight against noxious impulses coming from the object. It is a double front!

Urribarri: This definitely changes the transference.

Green: Of course, transference and transference interpretations. Winnicott will not say to his patient: "No, you project. You think that I am bad because you have the need for me to be bad." Winnicott will say, instead: "You are right, I am very bad."

Urribarri: I would like to make a technical observation, if you do not mind: You propose to interpret destructiveness, instead of what Winnicott does.

Green: Yes, but I think in what Winnicott proposes, there are some important things. When he says that it is important that the analyst can accept the projection, it is not about whether the patient can rectify his or her ideas, but whether the patient can live them.

Urribarri: Can he or she . . . ?

Green: . . . live them! As the number of people on the couch increased, so the psychoanalytic profile became more and more "parasitised" by non-neurotic structures. From then on, analysts started to realise that Freudian theory that was based on neuroses did not help them. And they turned their interest towards ego psychology in the USA, to Melanie Klein in England, to Lacan in France. They thought these new approaches were going to solve their problems. I think that these hopes ended up not being as beneficial as they were expected to be. So what I look for in my readings are authors who "talk to me". Those who give us an authentic contemporary thinking. Today, the question is no longer whether or not we agree with Freud. We have a new paradigm that is represented by certain authors; and maybe by some others, whom I happen not to know yet, because I cannot read them all. And also about what I have managed to contribute.

Urribarri: It seems to me that many colleagues, many readers, would say that if there is a new paradigm, it will be in the renewed working through and metabolisation of these issues that are displayed in your work.

Green: If you think so, it gives me great pleasure. I hope I have helped others. The important part is never to stop. To progress, to reflect, to tell oneself: yes, this seems important, we should keep it; this seems less important, we should set it aside.

Urribarri: In your works in the last few years, especially, we found an unprecedented and deep personal research of the analytic setting.

Green: I am glad that you refer to my own contributions. I think that in my last book [*Du Signe au discours,* 2011b] I realised that no analyst had given a true psychoanalytic description of what goes on in an analytic sessions. The description I present is, I think, one of the first to give a faithful account of how language works in a psychoanalytic session. The important thing is to understand that the analytic setting does make you speak in a different way. It is not about saying that in psychoanalysis one talks; it is about saying how one speaks, in which way. What are the effects of the patient's words on the patient and on the analyst himself? What modifications do the analyst's interpretations bring in the field of words? What shall we conclude?

1. that it is very important to give a true description of what goes on within the verbal exchange in an analysis;

2. that it is extremely important to make a language analysis accordingly to the specifics in psychoanalysis;

3. that we should question the concept of the setting because we know that there are patients who cannot accept the setting, and we are forced to do some other thing. Psychotherapy, face to face. We must deal with the positive effects of the setting and the failures of the setting. There is an enormous research field before us.

Notes

This interview by Fernando Urribarri was recorded in André Green's consulting room in May 2011, and the video was presented at the IPA Congress in Mexico in August of the same year. The present text of the interview is a translation for this edition of the subtitles of the original film, with substantial editing by Rosine Perelberg. A fuller interview was published by Ithaque, which contained the contents of two other conversations that took place later that year ["La Psychanalyse Contemporaine, Chemin Faisant 1960–2011: Vers un nouveau paradigme. Paris, May & October 2011", in F. Urribarri, *Dialoguer avec André Green* (pp. 101–127). Paris: Ithaque, 2013].

1. With the hypothesis of narcissistic libido and the extension of the concept of libido to the individual cells, the sexual instinct was transformed for us into Eros, which seeks to force together and hold together the portions of living substance. What are commonly called the sexual instincts are looked upon by us as the part of Eros which is directed towards objects. Our speculations have suggested that Eros operates from the beginning of life and appears as a 'life instinct' in opposition to the 'death instinct' which was brought into being by the coming to life of inorganic substance. These speculations seek to solve the riddle of life by supposing that these two instincts were struggling with each other from the very first" (Freud, 1920g, pp. 60–61n.).

References

Freud, S. (1917d [1915]). A metapsychological supplement to the theory of dreams. *Standard Edition, 14*: 217–236.

Freud, S. (1920g). *Beyond the Pleasure Principle. Standard Edition, 18*: 7–64.

Freud, S. (1926d [1925]). *Inhibitions, Symptoms and Anxiety. Standard Edition, 20*: 77–175.

Green, A. (1962). L'Inconscient freudien et la psychanalyse contemporaine. *Les Temps Modernes, 195*: 365–379.

Green, A. (1973). *Le Discours vivant*. Paris: Presses Universitaires de France. [*The Fabric of Affect and Psychoanalytic Discourse*. London: Routledge, 1999.]

Green, A. (1975). The analyst, symbolisation and absence in the analytic setting (on changes in analytic practice an analytic experience). *International Journal of Psychoanalysis, 56*: 1–22. Reprinted in: *On Private Madness* (pp. 30–59). London: Hogarth Press & The Institute of Psychoanalysis, 1986.

Green, A. (1980). Passions et destins des passions. Sur les rapports entre folie et psychose. *Nouvelle Revue de Psychanalyse, 21*. [Passions and their vicissitudes. In: *On Private Madness* (pp. 214–253). London: Hogarth Press & The Institute of Psychoanalysis, 1986.]

Green, A. (1983). *Narcissisme de vie. Narcissisme de mort*. Paris: Éditions de Minuit. [*Life Narcissism, Death Narcissism*. London: Free Association Books, 2001.]

Green, A. (1986). *On Private Madness*. London: Hogarth Press & The Institute of Psychoanalysis. [*La Folie privée. Psychanalyse des cas-limites*. Paris: Gallimard, 1990.]

Green, A. (1995). *Le Travail du négatif* . Bordeaux-Le-Bouscat: L'Esprit du Temps. [*The Work of the Negative*. London: Free Association Books, 1999.]

Green, A. (1999). On discriminating and not discriminating between affect and representation. *International Journal of Psychoanalysis, 80* (2): 277–316. Reprinted in: *Psychoanalysis: A Paradigm for Clinical Thinking*. London: Free Association Books, 2005.

Green, A. (2002). *La Pensée clinique*. Paris: Odile Jacob. [*Psychoanalysis: A Paradigm for Clinical Thinking*. London: Free Association Books, 2005.]

Green, A. (2007). *Pourquoi les pulsions de destruction ou de mort?* Paris: Éditions du Panama.

Green, A. (2011a). Les Cas limite. De La Folie privée aux pulsions de destruction et de mort. *Revue Française de Psychanalyse, 75*: 375–390.

Green, A. (2011b) *Du Signe au discours. Psychanalyse et théories du langage*. Paris: Éditions d'Ithaque.

Marty, P. (1976). *Les Mouvements individuels de vie at de mort*. Paris: Payot.

CHAPTER SEVEN

On clinical thinking: the extension of the psychoanalytic field towards a new contemporary paradigm

Fernando Urribarri

P sychoanalyst and historian Martin Bergmann was right when he said that Freud, for better or for worse, left behind a psychoanalysis that was far less definitive and complete, and more open to problems and developments, than his early disciples had believed. After Freud's death, his depth psychology met with good fortune in the rise of some original post-Freudian authors who made very valuable contributions, but also with the misfortune that each of these authors created a militant "school", proclaiming itself Freud's legitimate heir. The "three great post-Freudian dogmatisms", as Jean Laplanche (1987) calls them—ego psychology, Kleinianism, and Lacanianism—set up their own reductionistic model, converted it into a dogma, mechanised a particular technique, and presented an idealised leader as head of this school.

André Green's prolific work can be characterised as the search for a new contemporary psychoanalytic thinking, capable of overcoming the impasses and fragmentations of post-Freudian models.

In order to convey the significance and deep underlying unity beneath the apparent diversity and arborescence of André Green's work, I suggest that it is the question and theme of *"the contemporary"* that best defines his work, gives it its implicit unity, and brings it to life. From his 1962 paper on the Freudian unconscious and contemporary French psychoanalysis to his book, *Key Ideas for a Contemporary Psychoanalysis* (2005a), and then the posthumous *La Clinique psychanalytique contemporaine* (2012), Green's writings can be seen to be driven by the issue of the contemporary (as dialectically opposed to the Freudian and post-Freudian eras and models). Over this long journey—which I have witnessed since 2001 as his closest collaborator, participating in the conception and edition of each of his books—the notion of the contemporary evolves: from an adjective to a concept, from a question to a project, from an issue to a key idea for a new paradigm.

Green's epistemological engine is fuelled by the irreducible but fertile gap between Freudian foundations and the challenges of psychoanalytic practice with non-neurotic patients. According to Green, the contemporary project of building a new paradigm is very different from, and is in fact opposed to, the construction of yet another post-Freudian school or discourse. The contemporary project is a research programme, and André Green viewed his own work—as he wrote in *Key Ideas* (2005a)—as an important contribution to the foundations of a new contemporary paradigm: a new Freudian matrix, pluralist, extended, and complex.

Here I offer a panoramic picture of the evolution of Green's thought, focusing on the elaboration of his clinical thinking, which is at once original and representative of contemporary developments—developments that, according to André Green, have brought about a "silent revolution" in psychoanalytic practice in recent decades. Following this guiding thread, his clinical thinking, I hope to illustrate the Greenian research process, which moves from the extension of the psychoanalytic field to clinical practice with non-neurotic structures, to a proposal to construct a new contemporary psychoanalysis.

In order to describe the evolution of Greenian clinical thinking, I break it down into three main stages.

The first phase begins in 1975 with the Report he presented in London at the IPA Congress. Green formulates the contemporary psychoanalytic project, based on a historical vision of what he calls "the crisis of psychoanalysis". In this report, he proposes a programme of research into the possible variations and extensions of the analytic method required for treating borderline cases—cases in which the "action model" predominates. His study focuses on the functioning of the process of representation within the analytic setting[1] as a way to gauge the *limits of analysability.*

In the second phase, as a dialectical consequence of the first, Green (1980) proposes the need to return and elucidate the basic Freudian model. In a 1983 paper on language in psychoanalysis, Green (1984) puts forward an original theoretical model that spells out the fundamentals of the setting and the Freudian method for treating neurosis (Green, 1984) . There he suggests that *the dream is the implicit model for Freudian setting and clinical practice.*

The third stage dates from what Green calls the "turning-point of 2000": in his book *Key Ideas for a Contemporary Psychoanalysis* (2005a), he presents the contemporary project. In this context, and aiming to outline a general model for current psychoanalytic clinical practice, Green synthesises his two preceding models in the form of a *diptych comprised of the dream model and the action model* (correlated with neurotic and non-neurotic modes of functioning). This diptych allows for a reshaping of the fundamentals of the analytic technique, re-centred on the internal frame–external frame dialectic conceptual pair.

I hope that this schema sheds light on three different and important moments in Green's construction of contemporary clinical thinking: first, in terms of the analyst's mad thinking, defined by a self-aware borderline way of thinking about limits; second, in terms of the logic of heterogeneity and thirdness; and, finally, in terms of the analyst's psychic work and "the analyst's internal setting".

First stage:
the emergence of the contemporary project

The contemporary psychoanalytic project first emerged in André Green's work in the 1975 London Report: "The Analyst, Symbolisation and Absence in the Analytic Setting". The initial theoretical framework of this text is based on a new and resolutely anti-dogmatic historical and epistemological perspective, which translates into two concrete theses.

First, Green argues for the existence, currently, of a crisis in psychoanalysis stemming from internal and external factors. With regard to the internal factors, he stresses the changes taking place in analytic practice, which have led to a widening gap between technique and theory (even a fragmentation in several post-Freudian schools). Second, Green holds that in order to understand and confront these problems, it is necessary to think about them historically. He outlines three historical phases of a parallel evolution in analytic theory and technique, three movements with three corresponding models—namely Freudian, post-Freudian, and contemporary.

The Freudian model centres, from a theoretical point of view, on intrapsychic conflict, and, from a technical point of view on transference. The paradigmatic cases are those involving neuroses. In the post-Freudian model, the theory focuses on the relational or intersubjective dimension (with the emphasis placed on object relations in England or the role of the Other in France). The technique is reformulated around countertransference (or the analyst's desire). Here the sample cases involve psychosis (and children). The contemporary project, in its embryonic phase in 1975, focuses on the process of representation within the analytic setting, in order to assess borderline functioning. It aims to historicise and overcome the theoretical and clinical impasses reached in the Freudian and post-Freudian models.

In the conclusion to his London Report, Green writes:

> The solution to the crisis in which psychoanalysis finds itself does not lie within analysis alone. But analysis holds some cards with which its destiny will be played. Its future will depend on the way it finds in which to preserve its Freudian heritage while integrating its later acquisitions. [1975, p. 57]

This new research programme concentrates on borderline cases, seen as the new problem cases, the object of Green's study. Green defines these cases from a clinical (psychoanalytic) point of view as *situations or states at the limit of analysability,* rather than from a psychopathological point of view as *borderline cases.*

This theoretical perspective describes *representational functioning* in accordance with the theory of the heterogeneity of the psychoanalytic signifier, associating force and meaning, the economic and the symbolic. The introduction and the development of the concept of the frame (Bleger, Winnicott, Baranger, Donnet, Green) make it an analyser of analysability. To emphasise the significant change introduced by this theoretical elaboration, I suggest we use the concept of the frame instead of the terms previously coined by Freud and post-Freudian authors, in a more empirical fashion, as "the setting" and "the analytic situation".

Studying the limits of analysability implies redefining them. In 1975, Green introduces the key concept of the *analytic object*. The analytic object is a third, discursive, heterogenous object, made of representations and affects, the product of the meeting and the communication between the analyst and the analysand in the potential space of the setting. So analysability is re-defined in terms of the construction (or not) of the analytic object. This third object, understood as a sort of transitional object, expresses the potential and intermediary nature of the analytic space: the setting itself is considered to be a third element with a dimension that creates a third space. It constitutes the methodological device that allows for the production of analytic material, as well as the construction and study of the analytic object—a non-empirical, non-observational object. This then introduces a new triadic scheme into the analytic process: transference–countertransference–frame.

In this sense, contemporary clinical thinking emerges from the conceptualisation of the setting and the redefinition of analysability, constituting a new *logic of the analytic pair as a triadic structure*.

So it is not a surprise that the 1975 Report advocates a redefinition of the notion of countertransference, deviating from the post-Freudian version. Green points out the central role the analyst's tertiary processes have in establishing an interplay between primary and secondary processes. In addition to this innovative notion of tertiary process, his thinking is distinguished by an original conception of figurability and of the analyst's imagination. He reminds us that in Freud the implicit model of neurosis is founded on perversion (neurosis as the negative of perversion). At this point, post-Freudian authors began gradually moving their attention away from perverse fantasies and towards psychotic defence mechanisms. Green suggests that our listening should draw on a *double code* (psychosexuality and the work of the negative).

He thus introduces the notion of *private madness*, which, combining this double conflict in borderline cases, is revealed only in the transference. For this reason, he states, the analyst should be capable of an *analytic mad thinking*, in order to understand the singular logic behind the patient's private madness.

In this way, contemporary clinical thinking emerges and is consolidated primarily as a new form of analytic imagination: a borderline way of thinking (in the sense that Freud defines the drive as a borderline concept), a kind of a *self-aware borderline way of thinking about limits*, underpinned by "the analyst's mad thinking".

This research into the limits of analysability leads to the elaboration of an early theoretical model of borderline functioning, called the *double limit*. The process behind the elaboration of this model can be traced back to a series of articles published in the early 1980s—especially "Passions and Their Vicissitudes" (1980). As we shall see, in this article Green interweaves two tasks required of the analyst:

> The future of psychoanalytic theory, clinical work and technique does not lie in the replacement of Freudian concepts centered around castration with a modern concept concerned with other referents—fragmentation, disintegration, annihilation, etc.—but in the *articulation* of these two approaches to bridge the gap between them. [Green, 1980, p. 239]

We must return to the Freudian basic model and rethink it from our new experience with borderline cases to rediscover what Freud excluded from neurosis—namely, madness. It is from this new starting point, from this new territory whose boundaries are indistinct, that we will be able to look in both directions at the same time: in the direction of the neurotic structures and in the direction of the psychotic structures (Green, 1986, pp. 200–201).

Second stage:
the return to Freudian fundamentals

With his paper on language in psychoanalysis, Green (1984) fulfilled his promise to return to the fundamentals of the Freudian model and method for treating neurosis. From this method, Green deduces an original model for the functioning of analysis, the axis of which is a specifically psychoanalytic vision of language.

There are two main reasons for this return to basics. The first is *internal* to the very development of the Greenian project and stems from the study of borderline functioning within the setting. Green's research raises new questions that go beyond those posed by the double limit theory. Therefore, a *return to the basic model* is needed in order to uncover the relationship between the *drive-subject (intrapsychic) axis*, the *transference* (intersubjective), and the mediating (symbolising) role of language in analysis. For Green, as we said, the *model of the dream* is the implicit theoretical model in Freud's clinical work. This model, centred on the intrapsychic, needs to be articulated with the intersubjective dimension that arises from the psyche and the analytic process. This elaboration is made possible for Green thanks to his previous conceptualisation of the notion of framing structure.

This work results in an original metapsychological insight into the psychoanalytic setting (the first in the history of psychoanalysis, as far as we know) founded on the theory of symbolisation (re-defined by the triple representation and tertiary processes).

The second cause is *external* to the author's work. It coincides with the recent death of Lacan and an invitation Green received asking him to speak at a colloquium on language, commemorating the thirtieth anniversary of the Rome Discourse (Lacan, 1953). Green stated that it was only by doing this work that he was able to bridge the gap between his positive view of Lacan's theory and his negative view of Lacan's practice. Working to bridge this gap helped Green to understand both the coherence and the considerable limitations of Lacan's work. By redefining his own relationship to Lacan, he was able to consolidate his post-Lacanian identity in the theoretical sphere and develop his own model of the fundamentals and functioning of the analytic method.

The 1983 Report (Green, 1984) deconstructs the Lacanian system and goes on to construct an original model of the psychoanalytic process based on a metapsychology of the analytic frame as a matrix for symbolisation. Green accomplished this by addressing both the central question—and answer—that organise Lacan's model. "Why does the talking cure work? Because the unconscious is structured like a language." The Lacanian thesis, based on the application to psychoanalysis of Saussure's and Jacobson's linguistics, is countered by Green's specific theory of discourse and language in psychoanalysis, determined by the particulars of the frame and the transference. He states: "the analytic word unmourns language".

The frame is called the "language apparatus", since its aim is the most extreme transformation of psychic productions into language through free association. Because it is hypercathected by the transference, language functions as a mediator in the direction of what is not language—namely, the unconscious. The activation of the dynamic force of the thing-representation linked with the word-representation changes the status of the analytic discourse, and the analytic word becomes a "third" object, born of the communication between analyst and analysand. The frame itself is also considered as a third element (between analyst and analysand), and it is defined as the metaphorical representation and creation of a matrix for transitional and tertiary symbolisation:

> The frame brings together three polarities: the dream (narcissism), maternal care (the mother in Winnicott) and the prohibition of incest (the father in Freud). [Green, 1984, p. 123]

In other words,

> the function of the frame is to make possible a polysemic metaphorization. The psychoanalytical apparatus is able to give birth to what I call "the other of the object" (a figure of the first third object which may or not be the father) within a theory of generalised triangularity with a substitutable third. [Green, 1984, p. 121]

In the section on "The symbolic order: The tertiary process", Green writes:

> We postulate the existence of mechanisms which allow the primary and secondary process to relate to one another, in both directions: we call them tertiary processes and attribute them to the preconscious of the first "topographical scheme" and to the Ego of the second. Therefore the symbolic order is based not on language (as in Lacan) but on all the bindings/un-bindings/rebindings that operate in the agencies of the psychic apparatus. The tertiary processes form the bridge between the language apparatus (the frame) and the psychic apparatus. [1984, p. 146]

The fundamental practice of psychoanalysis
and clinical thinking

It is not surprising that some time after this return to, and renewal of, the foundations of the Freudian method, Green wrote his paper on the fundamental practice of psychoanalysis (1988), in which he tried to develop some of the consequences of his former work for clinical practice. In this paper one finds for the first time the expression (not yet a full concept) "clinical thinking" (*la pensée clinique*). We also find a new definition of the analytic process, based on the reflexive processes of subjectivation postulated in the Report—which are based on his theoretical model of the framing structure. He defines the analytic process as "the subject's return to himself via the detour of the resembling (significant) other" (1988, p. 571).

Concerning the analyst's mental functioning, he writes:

> If identification is considered to be the basis of the analyst's psychic work, the second factor corresponds to the figures that he produces. . . . From a general point of view the psychic activity of the analyst mobilizes and favours the process of representation [in French: "la *representance"*]; that is, the plural exercise of the different types and modes of representation. To produce meaning is to induce representations in the other. [Green, 1988, p. 582; translated for this edition]

All these formulations are articulated in another important paper on the psychic work of the analyst—centred in the tertiary process and the very important role that Green gives to preconscious functioning. In his 1986 paper on the capacity for reverie and the etiological myths he critically discusses the implicit theoretical models of post-Freudian techniques, in particular the Bionian notion of maternal reverie. At one point, arguing against a reductionistic Bionian tendency, he raises the question: "And what about the father's reverie?" He writes:

> What does the analyst's listening consist in? First, in understanding the manifest content of what is said, a necessary precondition for all that follows; then, and this is the fundamental stage, in *imaginarizing* the discourse: not only imagining it, but also including in it the imaginary dimension, construing what is implicit in such a discourse differently, in the mise-en-scène of understanding. In the following step, the analyst will unbind

the linear sequence of this chain by evoking other fragments of sessions: recent ones (perhaps of the last session), less recent ones (from months ago), and, finally, much older ones (such as a dream from the beginning of the analysis). The analyst has to be the archivist of the *history of the analysis* and search the records of his *preconscious memory;* to this end, he will call his associations to mind at all times. Such is the backdrop against which the analyst's capacity for reverie is developed. Such capacity grows in the final step, that of *rebinding,* which will be achieved by selecting and recombining the elements thus gleaned to give birth to the countertransferential phantasy, which is supposed to meet the patient's transferential phantasy. [Green, quoted in Urribarri, 2007, pp. 183–184; italics added]

In the quotation given above, I would stress that there is a technical shift from the classic (systematic) interpretation of transference to interpretation *in* the transference. The "here-now-with-me" dimension is thus articulated with the "there-then-with someone else". The Freudian *nachträglich* (the afterwardness, the *après-coup* that defines the specific temporal dimension of psychoanalysis) regains a central role, being elaborated in a dual way: as an essential dimension, inherent to the process of representation, and as a key to psychoanalytic work. Construction and "historisation" become key dimensions of the analytic work.

To the playful subject (postulated by Green in opposition to the Lacanian subject of the signifier, absorbed in combinatory and mathematical formalisations) responds a playful analyst, who is capable of operating in the different registers of the representational field, in accordance with an evolving transformational purpose. Directly inspired by the epistemology of self-organisation (Heinz Von Foerster, Francisco Varela, Henri Atlan), Green conceives of analysis as a poietic process following a sequence of organisation–disorganisation–reorganisation. That is to say, to paraphrase a Greenian formula, that the analytic process, like life, is a fertile disorder. At that point, clinical thinking becomes a logic of heterogeneity (Green, 1996) that fuels "tertiary thinking"—the specifically psychoanalytic form of the epistemology of complexity.

The revision of the fundamentals of the Freudian method that Green carried out in 1983 led to the development of different conceptual axes over the course of the following decade and the elaboration of new metapsychological fundamentals. Summarised very briefly, the new Greenian metapsychological foundations revolved around five main axes:

1. the drive–object pair, a *psychic atom* combining the intrapsychic and the intersubjective;
2. the general theory of representation, with its two aspects: one that enlarges Freudian theory to include the body, affect, and thought, and the other that corresponds to the framing structure as a matrix of symbolisation;
3. an expanded topographic model, based on the elaboration of the limit itself as a pivotal concept, which postulates the body and the real (external object) as dynamic spaces in a "double conflict" model.

And two meta-conceptual (or meta-psychoanalytic) axes:

4. thirdness—articulating a wide range of related concepts, from axiomatic open triangularity, to tertiary processes;
5. the work of the negative.

These last two meta-axes express Green's mature vision of the psyche as a heterogeneous, complex, open, conflictual process of the creation and destruction of psychic meaning. One can say that these five axes are the cardinal points of the contemporary clinical compass.

Third stage:
the turning-point of 2000 and the future of psychoanalysis

"The turning-point of 2000" is an expression used by André Green (2006) to describe the beginning of a new stage in the history of psychoanalysis and to evoke the idea of a new horizon. I suggest that it applies to his own work, given that, at this stage, his *implicit programme of research* had evolved into an explicit project aimed at overcoming the crisis of post-Freudian psychoanalysis by constructing a new contemporary paradigm. At this stage Green introduced the notion of clinical thinking as a new concept, or a new conceptual axis, that articulates both an epistemological and a technical dimension.

Speaking in 2000 at the International Colloquium on The Future of a Disillusion, Green asserts:

> Here is the programme on which we should reflect. We should forge pathways between the foundations of the psychoanalysis and the limits of the analysable, forcing our thought to move between contradictory polarities, to respond to the need to imagine today what analytic practice is, across the whole field and the various situations offered by the experience. [Green, 2000a, p. 46]

In order to underpin contemporary research, Green proposes building a theoretical–clinical matrix based on four main axes:

1. an updated reading of Freud, which reaffirms the value of metapsychology and the Freudian method as fundamentals of psychoanalysis;

2. a creative and critical appropriation of the main post-Freudian contributions (accompanied by a dialogue with contemporary authors from diverse schools of thought);

3. an extension of the psychoanalytic clinical field to include clinical practice with specific settings and variable frames for neurotic and non-neurotic structures;

4. a bridge with contemporary thinking and, above all, with complex epistemology.

In *Le Temps éclaté* [Shattered time], Green (2000b) proposes a new synthesis of the two previous models he developed, which now takes the form of a diptych composed of the *dream model* and the *action model*—a diptych that represents the heterogeneous totality of contemporary psychoanalytic practice, including neurotic and non-neurotic structures.

According to Green, the *dream/act* diptych opens up the possibility of a general reinterpretation of the fundamentals of analytic technique, revolving around another two dialectical conceptual pairs: the first composed of the representation processes and the unrepresented states, and the second of *external frame* and *internal frame*. The newly introduced notion of clinical thinking is, at its very core, the analyst's tertiary process, the underlying process that brings dynamic unity to the polarities of the dream/act diptych.

The dream and the act:
two Freudian models for contemporary clinical practice

The dream–act diptych is based on the extraction and elaboration of concepts derived from Freud's work. Both models deal directly with representation and its various statuses and functioning in the first and the second topography, respectively. These opposing models are correlated with neurotic and non-neurotic functioning. At the level of clinical thinking, this diptych introduces and thematises an articulation between the analyst's external and internal setting. As I wrote in 2004—in the context of my collaboration and dialogue with André Green—I think that the implicit theoretical model of Green's clinical thinking in general, and the implicit reference of this new diptych in particular, lies in his theory of the framing structure (Urribarri, 2005).

In the dream model, as a part of this diptych, the key aspect is that representations constitute a psychic (originary) starting point. The dream model centres on sexual desire, structured through fantasies and woven into representations. Clinical practice is founded on the compatibility between thing-representations and word-representations, transferentially articulated in free association. This corresponds to the psychoneurotic mode of functioning. It assumes that the containing function of the framing structure of primary narcissism is well enough established to allow the analysis to concentrate on the content, in accordance with a mainly intra-psychic conflict axis. This combination puts into play a tripod of relationships of transference and transformations between infantile neurosis, defence psychoneurosis, and transference neurosis. All in all, according to Green, within this model the analytic process is articulated within a triptych constituted by: frame/dream (telling of the dream)/interpretation.

The action model, in Green's view, is closely related to the second topography—characterised by the unconscious being replaced by the id. The action model originates in the movement of the drive. The latter can be linked to representation or can be evacuated through action. In other words, representation is a possible result, rather than a starting point. The action can take several forms (realised or not), but it always causes a short-circuit in symbolisation. In terms of the model of psychic functioning, deadly repetition compulsion takes the place of desire, while the experience of terror replaces the hallucinatory experience of satisfaction. Here, references to flaws in the relationship with the primal object and, simultaneously, with death narcissism are key. The framing structure, as a space for representation, is flooded by evacuative and/ or unbinding and disinvestment processes. The unrepresentable, therefore, bursts in on the analytic scene and puts a halt to both free association and free-floating attention.

In the action model, the interpretative axis centred on the intrapsychic should articulate with—and to some degree move towards—the intersubjective. The role of the *analyst-object* moves to the foreground of transference and technique—sometimes even literally, as in face-to-face treatments. The technical focus, therefore, shifts to the possibility of interiorisation during the session. The construction of the psychic continent and the preconscious as an internal transitional space becomes a necessary condition for the analysis of the contents. Before making the unconscious conscious, the manifest (whether it is acted or spoken) has to be made thinkable. For instance, analytic dialogue tries to create a kind of intersubjective preconscious fabric of representations. In this context, in terms of technique, the dream paradigm (of the interpretation of the latent content) is replaced by the playing model—the co-creation of the meaning, and its verbalisation in the intersubjective space as a necessary condition for its introjection into the ego.

The aim of analytic play is to achieve interiorisation during the session. Therefore, we must set our sights on the task of subjective appropriation. This entails prioritising what we can call, after Green, the *work of the limit, a particular and structurant work of the negative* with the aim of simultaneously building internal borders (that is, intermediate formations between psychic instances) and external borders (between the ego and the object). In the analyst's work, the representative function is associated with (and subordinate to) the framing function. In my own writings I have proposed that, in the action model, the analytic process is *organised* by a different triptych—the internal frame/the action/and analytic play—in the service of interiorisation and subjective appropriation (Urribarri, 2010).

On clinical thinking:
the analyst's psychic work and the analyst's internal setting

In *Psychoanalysis: A Paradigm for Clinical Thinking* (2005b), in order to define the specificity of analytic thinking, Green introduces the notion of *clinical thinking*, a concept that combines an epistemological dimension and a technical dimension. The clinical dimension concerns the "thinking-work" in the analytic relationship. In it, I have suggested, a conceptualisation of *the analyst's psychic work* emerged as a new conceptual axis (Urribarri, 2007).

Green revisits the concept of the frame and suggests that it is comprised of two distinct dimensions: a constant element and a variable element. Reversing the usual definitions, according to him, the variable element refers to all the conventional aspects of the setting and the contract, and the constant element of the analytic frame is the dialogical dimension co-created by the analytic relationship. This innovative formulation implies that the constant dimension of the analytic frame corresponds to the dynamic core composed of transference and countertransference movements, embedded within the rules of free association and free-floating attention. One of the major consequences of this vision is to deconstruct the common-sense orthodoxy that opposes (hierarchically) psychoanalysis and psychotherapy.

The study of the frame and its variations leads to the concept of *the analyst's internal frame*, at the core of contemporary clinical thinking. It is the analyst's internal frame that makes possible the transformations of the external frame. The previously established importance of the preconscious and the analyst's framing structure is now rediscovered as the foundation of the frame and its variations. Having in mind that the structuring frame is the key and implicit theoretical model for Green's clinical thinking, I would like to suggest that analytic technique—and therefore the analytic process—can be seen as successive (but non-lineal) movements of framing/de-framing/re-framing.

Contemporary psychoanalysis expands *the understanding of the analyst's psychic work* as a tertiary conceptual axis seeking to include free-floating attention and countertransference as partial and complementary dimensions of a complex process. Moreover, the importance of the analyst's imagination (particularly necessary when working at the limits of analysability) is emphasised. Redefined in this way, analytic listening emerges as wider than the countertransference, and the analyst's work goes beyond its working-through and use, as not every movement of the analyst's mind is countertransferential.

The *analyst's internal frame* is now conceptualised as a pre-conscious matrix for representation. Its optimum functioning is that of the tertiary processes (Green)—processes of binding and unbinding, the union and separation of heterogeneous elements and processes (primary and secondary, but also originary, archaic, semiotic, etc.) on which the analyst's understanding and creativity is based. In the working-through of the countertransference, the analyst's tertiary processes allow the primary unconscious resonance to link to memory traces and thus to acquire figurability, so that it can then be signified and thought through language, ready for its ultimate rebinding as thought within the analytic situation. The polysemic nature of the process implies that analyst's position is multiple and variable. It cannot be predetermined or fixed— neither as an oedipal father, nor as a mother-container, nor as a narcissistic double. The analyst must play (play ludically, and as in "perform"), according to the scripts at work in the polyphonic singularity of the analytic field. The acknowledgement that the unconscious "speaks" in many dialects requires, as an ideal, a "polyglot analyst"—as André Green remarkably exemplified it, both in his theory and in his practice.

I would like to end with a quotation from Green, speaking at the 2005 Colloquium on Unity and Diversity of Contemporary Psychoanalysis (Green, 2006): "The historians of psychoanalysis may mark the end of the beginning of the 2000s by designating in our discipline what I propose to call the turning-point of the millennium. Today, when some anxiously await the death of psychoanalysis, I, for one, see signs of a rebirth."

Note

1. Green uses the French word "*cadre*" (frame), to develop, in his own way, the notion introduced by the Argentinian author José Bleger—a word and a notion that is not synonymous with "setting", nor with "situation".

References

Green, A. (1962). L'Inconscient freudien et la psychanalyse contemporaine. *Les Temps Modernes, 195*: 365–379.

Green, A. (1975). The analyst, symbolisation and absence in the analytic setting (on changes in analytic practice an analytic experience). *International Journal of Psychoanalysis, 56*: 1–22. Reprinted in: *On Private Madness* (pp. 30–59). London: Hogarth Press & The Institute of Psychoanalysis, 1986.

Green, A. (1980). Passions and their vicissitudes. In: *On Private Madness* (pp. 214–253). London: Hogarth Press & The Institute of Psychoanalysis, 1986.

Green, A. (1984). *Le Langage dans la psychanalyse*. In: *Langages rencontres Psychanalytiques d'Aix-en-Provence 1983* (pp. 19–250). Paris: Les Belles Lettres.

Green, A. (1986). La Capacité de rêverie et le mythe étiologique. In: *La Folie privée. Psychanalyse des cas-limites*. Paris: Gallimard, 1990.

Green, A. (1988). La Pratique fondamentale de la psychanalyse. Vue de la Société Psychanalytique de Paris. Une conception de la pratique. *Revue Française de Psychanalyse, 52* (3): 569–593.

Green, A. (1996). La Representación y lo irrepresentable. Entretien avec Fernando Urribarri. *Revista Argentina de Psicoanálisis, 6* (Special issue, 1998/1999): 88–106.

Green, A. (2000a). Le Cadre psychanalytique. Son intériorisation chez l'analyste et son application dans la pratique. In: A. Green & O. F. Kernberg (Ed.), *L'Avenir d'une disillusion* (pp. 11–46). Paris: Presses Universitaires de France.

Green, A. (2000b). *Le Temps éclaté*. Paris: Minuit.

Green, A. (2005a). *Key Ideas for a Contemporary Psychoanalysis: Misrecognition and Recognition of the Unconscious*, trans. A. Weller. London: Routledge.

Green, A. (2005b). *Psychoanalysis: A Paradigm for Clinical Thinking*, trans. A. Weller. London: Free Association Books.

Green, A. (Ed.) (2006). *Unité et diversité des pratiques du psychanalyste. Colloque de la Société Psychanalytique de Paris*. Paris: Presses Universitaires de France.

Green, A. (2012). *La Clinique psychanalytique contemporaine*. Paris: Éditions d'Ithaque.

Lacan, J. (1953). The function and field of speech and language in psychoanalysis. In: *The Language of the Self*, trans. A. Wilden. Baltimore, MD: Johns Hopkins University Press, 1981.

Laplanche, J. (1987). Prologue. In: S. Bleichmar, *Aux Origines du sujet psychique*. Paris: Presses Universitaires de France.

Urribarri, F. (2005). Le Cadre de la représentation dans la psychanalyse contemporaine. In: F. Richard & F. Urribarri (Eds.), *Autour de l'œuvre d'André Green* (pp. 201–216). Paris: Presses Universitaires de France.

Urribarri, F. (2007). The analyst's psychic work and the three concepts of countertransference. In: A. Green (Ed), *Resonance on Suffering* (pp. 165–186). London: Karnac.

Urribarri, F. (2010). Postface. André Green: Passion clinique, pensée complexe. In: A. Green, *Illusions et désillusions du travail psychanalytique*. Paris: Odile Jacob.

ANDRÉ GREEN BIBLIOGRAPHY

Un Oeil en trop. Paris: Les Editions de Minuit, 1969. [*The Tragic Effect: The Oedipus Complex in Tragedy*. Cambridge: Cambridge University Press, 1979.]

Le Discours vivant. La conception psychanalytique de l'affect. Paris: Presses Universitaires de France, 1973. [*The Fabric of Affect and Psychoanalytic Discourse*. London: Routledge, 1999.]

L'Enfant de ça. Psychanalyse d'un entretien. La psychose blanche (with J.-L. Donnet). Paris: Editions de Minuit, 1973.

Narcissisme de vie. Narcissisme de mort. Paris: Minuit, 1983. [*Life Narcissism, Death Narcissism*. London: Free Association Books, 2001.]

Le Langage dans la psychanalyse. In: *Langages rencontres Psychanalytiques d'Aix-en-Provence 1983* (pp. 19–250). Paris: Les Belles Lettres, 1984.

La Folie privée. Psychanalyse des cas-limites. Paris: Gallimard, 1990. [*On Private Madness*. London: Hogarth Press & The Institute of Psychoanalysis, 1986.]

Que sais-je. Le Complexe de castration. Paris: Presses Universitaires de France, 1990, 2007.

La Déliaison. Paris: Les Belles Lettres, 1992.

Révélations de l'inachèvement. A propos du carton de Londres de Léonard de Vinci. Paris: Flammarion, 1992.

Un Psychanalyste engagé. Conversations avec Manuel Macias. Paris: Calmann-Lévy, 1994.

La Causalité psychique. Entre nature et culture. Paris: Odile Jacob, 1995.

Propédeutique. La métapsychologie revisitée. Seyssel: Champ Vallon, 1995.

Le Travail du négatif. Bordeaux-Le-Bouscat: L'Esprit du Temps, 1995. [*The Work of the Negative.* London: Free Association Books, 1999.]

Les Chaînes d'Eros. Paris: Odile Jacob, 1997. [*The Chains of Eros,* London: Karnac Books, 2002.]

La Diachronie en psychanalyse. Paris: Editions de Minuit, 2000.[*Diachrony in Psychoanalysis.* London: Free Associations, 2003]

Le Temps éclaté. Paris: Editions de Minuit, 2000. [*Time in Psychoanalysis.* London: Free Associations, 2002]

Idées directrices pour une psychanalyse contemporaine. Paris: Presses Universitaires de France, 2002. [*Key Ideas for a Contemporary Psychoanalysis. Misrecognition and Recognition of the Unconscious,* trans. A. Weller. London: Routledge, 2005.]

La Pensée clinique. Paris: Odile Jacob, 2002. [*Psychoanalysis: A Paradigm for Clinical Thinking.* London: Free Association Books, 2005.]

Hamlet et Hamlet. Une interprétation psychanalytique de la représentation. Paris: Bayard, 2003.

La Lettre et la mort. Promenade d'un psychanalyste à travers la littérature: Proust, Shakespeare, Conrad, Borges. . . . Entretiens avec Dominique Eddé. Paris: Denoël, 2004.

Love and Its Vicissitudes (with G. Kohon). London: Routledge, 2005.

Sortilèges de la séduction. Lectures critiques de Shakespeare. Paris: Odile Jacob, 2005.

Associations presque libres. Entretiens avec Maurice Corcos. Paris: Albin Michel, 2006.

Les Voies nouvelles de la thérapeutique analytique. Le dedans et le dehors. Paris: Presses Universitaires de France, 2006.

Pourquoi les pulsions de destruction ou de mort? Paris: Editions du Panama, 2007.

Joseph Conrad. Le premier commandement. Paris: Editions In Press, 2008.

Illusions et désillusions du travail psychanalytique. Paris: Odile Jacob, 2010. [*Illusions and Disillusions of Psychoanalytic Work.* London: Karnac, 2011]

La Clinique psychanalytique contemporaine. Paris: Editions d'Ithaque, 2012.

Penser la psychanalyse avec Bion, Lacan, Winnicott, Laplanche, Aulagnier, Anzieu, Rosolato. Paris: Editions Ithaque, 2013.

INDEX

space(s):
    blank, without representation, 2
    full or empty, in analyst's mind, 36
    negative, 91
    psychic, 27, 52
        re-shaping, 81, 87
    third, 18, 137
    and time:
        contraposition of, in art, 90
        representation of, xxiii, 90
spectrum of identity, 100
Spillius, E. B., xvii, 69
splitting, 6, 9, 20, 63, 125
    vs. repression, 2
    of single object, 5
    temporary, 10
SPP: *see* Société Psychanalytique de
        Paris
Stein, R., 8
Stern, D., xvi
Streeruwitz, A., xiii, xxi–xxvi
structural model of mind, 9, 10, 12,
        27, 29
subject and object:
    independence and interconnection
        of, 17–18
    lack of differentiation between,
        6, 86
subjectale, 17
sublimation, 47, 124
suicidal impulses, 17
superego, 7, 28
    concept of, 27, 35
symbolisation, 1–3, 16, 18, 26, 51, 64,
        65, 69, 111, 139, 143, 146
    primary, concept of, 10
    tertiary, 140
symbolism, dream, 8

talking cure, 139
Taylor, S. W., xvi
temporality(ies):
    multiple, 96, 97
    and thirdness, Green's concept of,
        18–19
tertiary process(es), 137, 139–141, 143,
        145, 148
    preconscious links supporting, 15

tertiary thinking, 142
Theseus, 106–109
thing-representation, 119, 140, 145
thinking deficits, 68
third, crucial relevance of, in
        psychoanalytic theory, 18
thirdness, 24, 37, 52, 135, 143
    in psychoanalytic process, 18
    and temporality, Green's concept
        of, 18–19
third object, analytic object like, 18
third space, 18, 137
thought/thinking:
    compulsion to, 14, 85
    origins of, theory of, 3
    paralysis of, 6
time:
    concept of, 95
    entering, 81, 87
    linear understanding of, 97
    and space:
        contraposition of, in art, 90
        representation of, xxiii, 90
timelessness, in unconscious, 91
Tóibín, C., 98, 99
topographical model of mind, 8, 10,
        26, 29
totalitarianism, 35
transference, 30–31, 53, 62, 65, 69, 129,
        136–140, 145–147
    dead mother awakened and
        animated in, 15
    double, 25
    interpretation in, 15, 18, 29, 55, 58,
        138, 142
    interpretation of, 29
    narcissistic, 17
    negative, 122
    object in, 18
    revelation of, dead mother as, 14
    role of, 3
transference depression, 14
transference interpretations, 129
transference neurosis, 4, 145
transformation, 75–88
transitional object, 137
transitional phenomena, 21
transitional space, 146